ANYONE CAN / EVERYONE MUST

Issuing the Clarion Call for
The Church to Fulfill the Great Commission

AC Curtis

THE OBJECT AND OBJECTIVE OF MISSIONS
THE STATE OF THINGS TODAY

Introduction

Throughout the world there is a strong hunger for the tandem of freedom and peace; the price of which many times comes on the backpacks of soldiers. There is a new backpack being introduced, however, to those seeking such freedom and peace—the backpack of the daring missionary. John Wesley once said, "Give me 100 men who hate nothing but sin and fear nothing but God ..." and it's these men and women who have adopted that slogan and abandoned their own convenience and comfort for a direct alignment to God's passionate dream. This is a book dedicated to them and to the possibility that there might be more of them. Where can we find them? We need look no further than the very entity created by Jesus Himself—the Church.

Congruent to the needs of billions of people around the world is an inspirational rise of the call of God to His bride, the Church, to engage in an all-points-bulletin pursuit of lost people everywhere. God has issued an Amber Alert for each lost child and will not stop until they are found. He is employing and imploring His children who are safely tucked away in His kingdom to join His massive worldwide search. He is trimming all the excess baggage that so many of His children are carrying to make their deployments more streamlined and effective. He is hoisting the sails of each church's flagships to breathe a fresh gust of His Holy Spirit wind in an all-out attempt to get those "ships" headed due-course for lost humanity. This book is that clarion call to the Church to get out of the pleasure boats of life and out into the waters of missions and evangelism.

**ANYONE OF US CAN—IF WE WILL.
EVERYONE OF US MUST—BEFORE IT'S TOO
LATE.**

THE OBJECT AND OBJECTIVE OF MISSIONS

"World missions was on God's mind from the beginning."

Dave Davidson

Psalm 67

1 May God be merciful and bless us. May His face smile with favor on us. 2 May Your ways be known throughout the earth, Your saving power among people everywhere. 3 May the nations praise You, O God. Yes, may all the nations praise You. 4 Let the whole world sing for joy, because You govern the nations with justice and guide the people of the whole world. 5 May the nations praise You, O God. Yes, may all the nations praise You. 6 Then the earth will yield its harvests, and God, our God, will richly bless us. 7 Yes, God will bless us, and people all over the world will fear Him.

The Object

Let's just cut right to the chase—the *object* of missions is one Person—Jesus Christ. (Colossians 1:13-20) He is the exclusive focus of the entire universe, and every creature in His universe exists to exalt Him, that is except for two—human beings and fallen angels (demons). This is simply inexcusable! Human beings hold the same infamous reputation as demons. Yet, God does not love demons nor seek to rescue them, only us.

Looking closely at Psalm 67 we see how much God is deserving of honor and praise, and how much getting His honor out to all the nations has been His focus since time began. His redemptive power and purpose has reverberated vociferously throughout the chronicles of time and history, and He hasn't changed His mind.

Notice verses 2 and 3: "May Your ways be known throughout the earth, Your saving power among people everywhere. May the nations praise You, O God. Yes may all the nations praise You." I have to announce a wonderful revelation—Jesus receives the greatest, most genuine praise from the lips of those who have just been rescued. The song of the redeemed is the greatest, most heartfelt worship song there is. Think about it, what kind of thanks and praise and honor does a person give to the hero that just snatched them away from the clutches of death right at the last moment? Or, what kind of accolades does a basketball player at any level receive who hits the last basket at the buzzer to win the championship for his team? Jesus is and will always be the greatest hero the world has ever seen, if they get to see Him before the judgment.

God desires to be known in every continent, every country, and every town or village in the world. He also wants to be known for who He is. His fame is on the line; His name is to be heard from every mouth, preferably in a manner of praise, because that is what He is genuinely due.

The Objective

If Jesus is the *object* of missions, then the Gospel represents the *objective*. The Gospel is the pure and undefiled "good news" of what Jesus did for all of mankind. There is nothing so sacred, nothing as altruistic as the Gospel. The Gospel is the one and only Message that the Lord is constantly promoting and endorsing. So much of what the enemy (the devil) tries to do is to hinder the spreading of this good news. He works overtime to discredit those who embrace the Gospel and is supremely diligent at diluting the importance of the Gospel.

My family and I live in the mid-south region of the U.S., and so we don't get a ton of winter weather. Usually, about once a year, we will experience that which people in the northern states have come to abhor—snow. When snow does come unexpectedly to our region, my six children absolutely go crazy! They wake up looking out of the windows of their bedrooms and start with the "oohs" and "aahs" as they greet the day. We cannot wait long before we are putting gloves, hats, and thick coats on to get to play in the beautiful white stuff before the first bit of sun begins to melt it away.

One day recently we had one of those unexpected snow days, and I stepped out into my front yard now blanketed with perfect "whiteness." I scooped up a ball of snow into my hand and looked at the perfection of it. I even ate some. I ate it because I knew it was pure and undefiled. Then, it hit me. This is what the Gospel is—perfect like driven snow. It is perfect in its origin, *from above*, that is until we, *down here*, begin to trample on it, handle it, and misrepresent it. When this happens, the Gospel from our perspective becomes tainted and no longer purely white. We do not have this right. The Gospel should never be tainted nor trifled with, and it easily stands alone in its effectiveness and power. (Romans 1:16-17)

I love the Gospel. I love Who it came from, what it stands for, and what it has done in my life and in the lives of billions of people on every continent, in every country, and in *nearly* every people group.

We should make Jesus our object and disseminating His Gospel our objective. When we take that approach to missions, we can begin to see exponentially productive results.

II Corinthians 5:18-20

18 And all of this is a gift from God, who brought us back to himself through Christ. And God has given us this task of reconciling people to him. 19 For God was in Christ, reconciling the world to himself, no longer counting people's sins against them. And he gave us this wonderful message of reconciliation. 20 So we are Christ's ambassadors; God is making his appeal through us. We speak for Christ when we plead, "Come back to God!"

There might be a number of different strategies for effectively spreading and advancing the Gospel, from humanitarian relief to church-planting, but there is one ideal, one purpose— putting everything we have into reconciling human beings back to their Creator for their sake and His honor.

I try to help persuade believers about two things concerning their existence:

1.- They were created to be in heaven with God forever; and
2.- They are alive in order to bring as many as possible with them to heaven before they die.

This sounds supremely simple, yet so many of us make it supremely complicated. We are not on this earth to save the planet or encourage a few people, or even to accomplish great things. We are simply here to receive His merciful and free gift of eternal life, and offer it right away to as many as possible.

I have been a believer for 20 years and have fallen down on my "job" as "messenger of reconciliation" many times. God has gracefully forgiven me, but continues to remind me of my purpose for living. At times He has gently reminded me with a quiet whisper in my heart of my need to be focused on one thing—reaching souls for Him. At other times He has had to resort to more stern tones and warnings through very graphic and horrifying dreams of hell to illustrate the seriousness I needed to embrace for the sake of millions. Those are times you wake up and nothing else in life seems to matter, for you are now on a mission to "empty hell and populate heaven" and nothing and no one should be allowed to stop you.

In addition, I try to convince Christians of two beliefs that are imperative to their Christian walk:

1.- God wants every person in heaven; and
2.- God needs believers to get them there.

We will talk about this in some detail later, but I have to say that I have witnessed so many believers who have yet to adopt this two-fold belief. They have arrogantly "decided" to embrace philosophies and ideologies that support their "right to choose" whether or not they will get involved in the task of the Great Commission. This is both criminal and tragic, and Jesus is not at all amused. His heart aches for the masses of humanity who do not know Him. He wants them each to be with Him forever, as was His original intent, and calls out to His Church to be solely responsible for the task at hand.

One day there will be no more need for this thing called *missions*. One day, when God the Father decides to start "wrapping things up," chaos will break loose on planet earth (Matthew 24:29-31), and each person alive will begin to cry out in mortal anguish at having not received their "one shot" at eternal life. Sounds like we have a clear objective until that day—missions.

THE STATE OF THINGS TODAY

"The command has been to go, but we have stayed—in
body, gifts, prayer, and influence."

Robert Savage

Are we doing a good job of bringing honor to the Person of Jesus Christ by advancing His Gospel, especially where it has yet to take root? Are we actively reaching lost people? Are we fulfilling the Great Commission? Some in the Church would say yes, while others might strongly contend otherwise. Whatever your personal take might be, the truth remains that we have much work to do and it is time to begin doing it.

The truth is that in many ways a large portion of the Church today is getting on board with God's great command to go. I've seen many churches that are committed to reach the lost both directly around them and throughout the world. One such church is actually lead by my dear friend and pastor, David Jett. He pastors Crossgates Baptist Church in Brandon, Mississippi. His heart for the Lord and for missions is unequaled. Pastor Jett believes that the more intimate you become with the Savior, the more you can't help but get out and tell everyone about Him. A person who visits Crossgates will most likely come away with two things:

1.- The members there love to worship freely; and
2.- They hate for lost people to go to hell.

You find it plastered on the hallways as you wind around their facility—ministry to different lost segments of society. The church under Jett's tutelage is flourishing; not just because of his great *leadership*, but because of their great *partnership*. You see, in order to be the kind of church that radically transforms society by winning the lost of that society, the majority of the members must adopt, embrace, and become individual stewards of just such an ideology. We will tackle this subject in more detail later.

Though there are many churches much like Crossgates who are listening to the heartbeat of the Lord, embracing His Great Commission, and abandoning themselves to His call, there are so many more who are not. A very large contingent of the Church in America seems greatly challenged by the idea and ideal of missions; thus the reason for writing this book. It is my hope that people begin taking seriously the mandate we have all been given. This mandate is the highest priority on our Savior's "to do list" before He comes back—win the world!

The Church Must Rediscover Its Original Intent

God is the Master Architect and Builder of the greatest design in history—His Church. He has the original blueprints and has mapped out a specific purpose for utilizing such a valuable entity. So, what exactly is that intent? According to hermeneutical theory, when studying a subject in the Bible, you must remember to apply the law of first mention. This simply says, "What was the context of the first time the word was mentioned?"

In addition, when studying the Bible, it is important to remember how often a word, subject, or phrase is used, and what is the common denominator of its meaning and purpose.

The word "church" or ekklesia (*ek-klay-see'-ah*) is a gathering of believers. The first time in all of Scripture it is mentioned is by Jesus Himself in Matthew 16:18. *"Now I say to you that you are Peter (which means rock) and upon this rock I will build My church, and all the powers of hell will not conquer it!"*

Now this is not to suggest that Jesus was saying the Church was to be a militant army bent on destruction. It is, however, meant to convey the first, simple function of the Church—to advance the kingdom of Christ against the kingdom of Satan. Is the Church today doing a masterful job of that? Probably not. There may be many reasons for this, but I believe it gets down to one fundamental problem: the devil is serious and on the attack and the Church is not.

To discover common denominators for the word "church" we must look at what is "normative" in Scripture. Normative simply means *what is said most often about that word or subject or phrase in context.*

Following are three "normative" features about the Church which are clearly illustrated in the book of Acts:

1.- The Church was active and full of miraculous power *(Acts 2:1-12; 2:42-43; 3:1-11; 4:29-31; 5:12-16)*;
2.- The Church was strongly persecuted *(Acts 5:17-19; 7:57-60; 8:1-3; 11:19*; and
3.- The Church was a sending force for missions *(Acts 11:22; 12:1; 13:1-4; 14:23; 15:3-4; 15:22-30; 15:41).*

Additionally, you need only look at the activities of the main characters of the book of Acts to understand their purpose and focus. It was simple—*spread the Message everywhere that Jesus is the only Savior for mankind.* Men such as Paul and Peter, together with their fellow sold-out missionary friends, John, Barnabas, Luke, Matthew, Silas, James, Phillip, Stephen, Epaphroditus, Tychicus, John Mark, Timothy, Titus; women such as Mary, Martha, Priscilla; and many others were completely married to the cause of Christ for His Church to preach the Good News to everyone everywhere. In fact, they gave up their very lives for advancement of the Gospel.

So, we might be able to conclude that God's original intent for the Church was **to make a supernaturally powerful and active group of committed believers bent on advancing and establishing the Gospel throughout the world.**

In your analysis, how are we doing? Are we fulfilling that call? How close, in your personal assumption, is your own church to the original blueprint? How about you and your family?

In understanding that God has called me and my family to be devoted to *motivating, mobilizing*, and *moving* people to their mission field, I've noticed two main responses that reveal part of the problem. I call them *the greenhouse effect and draft dodgers.*

The Greenhouse Effect

Basically, this is a philosophical approach to local church ministry by church leaders and churches in general. It follows this pattern of thought: "God has given the people in our congregation to us and we should keep them." Now, it is true that we should do our best to try to *maintain* people who come to Christ in an all-out attempt to keep them from abandoning the faith. What we should not do, however, is *hoard* them. The truth is that God sends people to us so that we can *love* them, *train* them, *equip* them, *empower* them, and begin *releasing* or *sending* them.

We cannot put systems into place that keep people inoculated against the problems in the world while we pour nutrients into them which were intended to prepare them for ministry to the world.

The whole discipleship idea is a means to two ends (Ephesians 4:11-16):

1.- Maturity of the believer for the sake of the Church; and
2.- Maturity of the Church for the sake of the world.

We should follow that same pattern in order to achieve the results God desires. Believers need a healthy balanced dose of sanctification coupled with opportunities to bring others to Christ. In other words, we should encourage believers to *sanctify* while they *testify*. We will discuss this some later.

Sometimes the best evangelists are those who just recently received Christ. Each of our churches will benefit greatly when we recognize this and offer new believers missions opportunities instead of chaining them to ideologies that lock them in the greenhouse.

Draft Dodgers

Every person who receives Christ as their Savior also receives Him as their Commander in Chief in a war that will rage on until

He returns. Jesus wants and needs to be both personal rescuer and boss of each of our lives.

Nonetheless, many believers today, though knowing that Jesus commands them to go, are refusing to adhere to that command. These are the *draft dodgers*. They refuse to go and fight to rescue perishing millions of lost, hurting, unreached people by declaring personal excuses such as *lack of ability* and *fear of the unknown*. They even may go as far as to reinterpret the Scriptures, diluting the emphasis that Jesus and the early church put on missions and evangelism. These excuses may make the grade with their leaders, their families, and their friends, but not with their Commander—Jesus.

At the outset of World War II our proud and prosperous nation pooled every resource and every available man to begin mobilizing toward a concerted effort to defeat the enemy. Twenty years later, during the Vietnam War, it became en vogue to resist the authorities of this once proud country and defy them to send anyone to fight. Though the cause was worthy (one nation trying to rescue another nation), the resistance was much more popular; thus, two nations, Vietnam and Cambodia, were scorched and scarred beyond words. Who could forget the images of the Pol Pot and Khmer Rouge lead massacre of hundreds of thousands of Cambodians in the "Killing Fields" directly following the American military pullout in 1975? Equally tragic were the images in 1976 and 1977 of the thousands of boat people from Vietnam begging for international help as they fled the Communist takeover in their country? They held out their feeble hands while the international community and the Church in the West for the most part pitied them but took little responsibility.

I sincerely believe many draft dodgers in the Body of Christ will one day have to gaze upon, at the Day of Judgment, the many thousands they could have reached but chose not to.

Before we start handing out grades (which is not my intent), we need to look at some of the broader issues that stand in the way. Following are several issues I believe are stonewalling mission efforts across the board which the Church faces today.

Church Fragmentation

This epidemic is worldwide in the Church. Christians seem to have forgotten the prayer of Jesus in John 17. In this prayer Jesus reveals some of His deepest sentiments toward the Church, and His greatest desire: "that they would all be one, just as You and I are one—as You are in Me, Father, and I am in You." (verse 21)

1 After saying all these things, Jesus looked up to heaven and said, "Father, the hour has come. Glorify your Son so he can give glory back to you. 2 For you have given him authority over everyone. He gives eternal life to each one you have given him. 3 And this is the way to have eternal life—to know you, the only true God, and Jesus Christ, the one you sent to earth. 4 I brought glory to you here on earth by completing the work you gave me to do. 5 Now, Father, bring me into the glory we shared before the world began. 6 "I have revealed you to the ones you gave me from this world. They were always yours. You gave them to me, and they have kept your word. 7 Now they know that every-thing I have is a gift from you, 8 for I have passed on to them the message you gave me. They accepted it and know that I came from you, and they believe you sent me. 9 "My prayer is not for the world, but for those you have given me, because they belong to you. 10 All who are mine belong to you, and you have given them to me, so they bring me glory. 11 Now I am departing from the world; they are staying in this world, but I am coming to you. Holy Father, you have given me your name;[b] now protect them by the power of your name so that they will be united just as we are. 12 During my time here, I protected them by the power of the name you gave me.[c] I guarded them so that not one was lost, except the one headed for destruction, as the Scriptures foretold. 13 "Now I am coming to you. I told them many things while I was with them in this world so they would be filled with my joy. 14 I have given them your word. And the world hates them because they do not belong to the world, just as I do not belong to the world. 15 I'm not asking you to take them out of the world, but to keep them safe from the evil one. 16 They do not belong to this world any more than I do. 17 Make them holy by your truth; teach them your word, which is truth. 18 Just as you sent me into the world, I am sending them into the world. 19 And I give myself as a holy sacrifice for them so they can be made holy by your truth. 20 "I am praying not only for these disciples but also for all who will ever believe in me through their message. 21 I pray that they will all be one, just as you and I are one—as you are in me, Father, and I am in you. And may they be in us so that the world will believe you sent me. 22 "I have given them the glory you gave me, so they may be one as we are one. 23 I am in them and you are in me. May they experience such perfect unity that the world will know that you sent me and that you love them as much as you love me. 24 Father, I want these whom you have given me to be with me where I am. Then they can see all the glory you gave me because you loved me even before the world began! 25 "O righteous Father, the world doesn't know you, but I do; and these disciples know you sent me. 26 I have revealed you to them, and I will continue to do so. Then your love for me will be in them, and I will be in them."

There is no more serious issue in the Church today than this. Conversely, there is not a more productive way to reach the entire world than for the Church to put aside the trivial non-essentials and commit to being *ecumenical.* Jesus not only endorses it and commands it, but He prays earnestly for it. In response to this, what then do you think we should do?

Additionally, we discover that this fragmentation comes from a source that is not the least bit heavenly, and yet comes at a cost that is every bit eternal.

Let's look at some passages from I Corinthians 1:10-13:

10 I appeal to you, dear brothers and sisters, by the authority of our Lord Jesus Christ, to live in harmony with

*each other. Let there be no divisions in the church. Rather,
be of one mind, united in thought and purpose. **11** For some
members of Chloe's household have told me about your
quarrels, my dear brothers and sisters. **12** Some of you
are saying, "I am a follower of Paul." Others are saying,
"I follow Apollos," or "I follow Peter," or "I follow only
Christ." **13** Has Christ been divided into factions? Was I,
Paul, crucified for you? Were any of you baptized in the
name of Paul? Of course not!*

There are some trivial matters that foster intense fragmentation in the Body of Christ. These "matters" anger the Lord, stain
His reputation, and push millions into a Christ-less eternity! I think
we should be willing to get rid of them at all cost. Here are just a
handful of those matters:

a.- The manner in which someone is baptized;
b.- Whether or not Christians will go through the tribulation;
c.- What time Jesus will return;
d.- What deems a church worship service appropriate; and
e.- Whether or not signs and wonders are for today.

Some years ago (1984), the very controversial and often vulgar
musician and songwriter Bob Geldof managed to pull together
dozens of musicians for production on a song entitled "Do they
know it's Christmas" and subtitled "Feed the World". The idea
behind such a production was to bring awareness to and raise
support for the tragic plight of the people of Ethiopia. Geldof set
out to get some of the highest profile singers and musicians in all
of the UK for this unforgettable production. He paid to have each
of them come and devote their talents to this one noble cause.
This group became known as Band-Aid and helped to spawn an
amazing movement which culminated in the following year's Live-
Aid concert.

Here's the point: a lost person spent everything he had to rally
as many people as he could to help offset the incredible suffering
of millions of people. Here's the sub-point: each of the singers and

musicians had their own agents, their own careers, and their own image to uphold. Yet each rallied around one cause for at least one time and put their personal careers on hold to accomplish it. Wow! And none of them were believers. Having just recently returned from a trip to Ethiopia, I saw with my own eyes that although this country has recovered somewhat from the famine of the early '80s, it is still suffering today. On that trip I also paid close attention to stories of the adult survivors of the three-year famine in Ethiopia. I remembered that many historians had called this the single greatest natural disaster in history. Without question, my heart was broken that the Church did not rally and pool all of its great resources and people together and outdo the efforts of Bob Geldof and Band-Aid.

Our Lovely Labels

When we name our churches we do so in an attempt to tell "saved" people what kind of church we are—*doctrinally*. This way, I guess, we figure we won't have to contend with problems. The problem with that thinking is that we aren't heeding one of the key doctrines in the Church—*unity*.

Now, this is not to suggest giving ground to obvious doctrinal error that can pull us away from Jesus and from the truth of Scripture. II Timothy 3:14-4:4 gives a distinct warning against just such a thing:

> *14 But you must remain faithful to the things you have been taught. You know they are true, for you know you can trust those who taught you. 15 You have been taught the holy Scriptures from childhood, and they have given you the wisdom to receive the salvation that comes by trusting in Christ Jesus. 16 All Scripture is inspired by God and is useful to teach us what is true and to make us realize what is wrong in our lives. It corrects us when we are wrong and teaches us to do what is right. 17 God uses it to prepare and equip his people to do every good work.*
>
> *1 I solemnly urge you in the presence of God and Christ Jesus, who will someday judge the living and the dead*

*when he appears to set up his Kingdom: **2** Preach the word*
of God. Be prepared, whether the time is favorable or not.
Patiently correct, rebuke, and encourage your people with
*good teaching. **3** For a time is coming when people will no*
longer listen to sound and wholesome teaching. They will
follow their own desires and will look for teachers who will
*tell them whatever their itching ears want to hear. **4** They*
will reject the truth and chase after myths.

However, we must be so careful not to contend for something
that is trivial and non-essential. A great plumb line for this is, of
course, the actual Word of God itself. We must commit to knowing
it and understanding what God meant by what He had written
down in the Bible. Rule of thumb here: if you want to know the
true meaning of what has been written or said by someone (in this
case—the Lord), go straight to the one who said it or wrote it.
Simple.

In addition, unity does not suggest complete *uniformity*. We are
obviously very different in our experiences, cultural backgrounds,
education, etc., but the celebration of such differences centered
around one key thing—the Gospel, and one key person—Jesus,
actually brings unity. Abandonment of this fundamental truth is
likened to the abandonment of breathing. None of us can exist or
function without breath, yet we far too often hold tightly to ideas
and concepts that produce anything but unity.

What an amazing affront to God's leadership of the Church!
We are to be under His headship, and yet we fight about so many
things that seem to fracture every bone in His Body. All of this is
done while millions perish without ever seeing the Light that we
boast lives in us. What a tragedy and what a shame!

In order to right this wrong and turn the ship, I strongly believe
that churches need to commit to having at least three ecumenical
and multi-racial services per year. That's one per quarter. Think
about it. What would your own church, your own life, your own
ministry look like if you committed to this; one service per quarter
blending worship styles, preaching, and overall precious fellowship? What a utopia!

First of all, God would begin smiling on you and your family and church in an unprecedented way. He is looking for this and longing for it. Just imagine if you committed to it. What blessings would overtake you! What favor!

Secondly, you would begin bridging differences in your community in a dramatic and lasting fashion. Think what it would look like to a lost community when your church starts reaching across aisles of petty differences to build *common-unity*. Notice the word exchange. They would knock the doors down to get to you.

Thirdly, you would be sending a loud message to all lost people around you that the Church genuinely cares about them because it demonstrates such care toward its own. Often lost people say, "Why believe in Jesus when those who say they follow Him don't get along?" And who in the world can blame them? Today in many churches you get into as many fights as you would in a bar. Why go through that? Why put your family in harm's way and waste a good "day off"? Yet, despite the churches that act in this way, there is a remnant of churches rising out of the ashes of terrible publicity to interact with their culture in a loving and appealing way. They will stand out as beacons of light in a dark and twisted world, and perhaps win many through their efforts.

Multiple Distractions

This, too, is huge. The devil, in all of his conniving trickery, is working overtime at getting us to fight and divide, but if that doesn't pan out well for him, he'll work even harder at plan B—*distracting the believers*. And distracted we are! We are distracted by prosperity and exclusivity, legalism and license, over-indulgence and under-productivity. One comparative look at the churches in America to the persecuted and impoverished churches overseas might illustrate a clear point—the American church is distracted nearly to sleep! We have been lulled to sleep by so many different factors. I believe I John 2:16-17 gives us a simple expla-nation as to why.

16 For the world offers only a craving for physical plea-sure, a craving for everything we see, and pride in our achievements and possessions. These are not from the Father, but are from this world. 17 And this world is fading away, along with everything that people crave. But anyone who does what pleases God will live forever.

What are some of the factors that distract us today?

"For the world offers only a craving for physical pleasure..."

Pursuit of Our Own Personal Desires and Dreams

Many of us have been taught since we were young to "look out for number one." Somehow, I think some of us bought into that then and have since dragged it into our new relationship with Christ. We just can't seem to put down this precious baggage. Why? Because we are naturally inclined to pursue pleasure. We don't like pain or suffering or even remote discomfort. In addition, we understand what it is that will make us live better, more plea-surable lives, and we believe that we are entitled to that. There are two fundamental problems with this theory:

1.- The pleasure of this life is a complete counterfeit to the true pleasure found only in an intimacy with our Creator. (Psalm 16:11)
2.- The pleasure of this life always leaves us wanting more because it never satisfies. (I Peter 1:24)

As each of us pursues his/her own pleasure, our dreams follow those desires. How many times do you hear someone say, "I am chasing God's dream, not mine"? Rarely, if ever. Again, early in life we are taught that "we can be anything we want." This builds our self-esteem, but leaves us completely unfulfilled. We were created for God's good pleasure and for His dreams. He has a will that He wants obeyed and a dream that He longs to be fulfilled—

namely the Great Commission. I often hear people say that they are surrendered to God's will, yet I see them chasing *their* dreams, not *His*. I don't believe we have that right. Conversely, we do have the distinct *privilege* of honoring our Great Master and Savior by pursuing His dreams.

"...a craving for everything we see..."

Lack of Personal Contentment

Contentment is a challenge to our culture today. We are bombarded nearly every minute of each day with a value system of the world which says, "You haven't arrived until you have this." We buy into it because we are simply looking for bigger and better. Why do we do that when we have access to the Biggest and the Best there is—Jesus? We could choose to have these cravings and longings for "more" swallowed up by His great presence and purpose. We lose so much because we just don't *see* Him and very rarely *feel* Him. However, if by faith we focus on Him, we can then begin seeing Him for all that He is and for all that He alone can bring us. Contentment begins and is sustained from that point.

"...and pride in our achievements and possessions."

Desire to be Exalted

Can you imagine that first sinful moment of pride spawned by Lucifer in heaven? What audacity and foolishness! How could any being in all of the universe think that they could ascend to the throne of the Creator of that universe? How could that which is created ever be able to lift up a hand or thought against the One who created it and could certainly destroy it? Notwithstanding, that is exactly what the devil did. It is sad to think that so many of us follow in those ultra-foolish footsteps! This world does its dead-level best at helping to foster such pride. Kings and leaders the world over and throughout history have tried their hand at this mirage of self-exaltation and have wound up face down in their own pitiful bewilderment.

Indeed, in comparison, the Church has struggled with this search for exaltation in its history as well. The Church does not need to self-exalt, but Christ-exalt. God is looking to exalt the Church if it will oblige Him and humble itself.

There may be other distractions as well. The key is to under-stand some of those, repent, and begin moving toward more focused, single-minded goals and systems that bring a smile to the face of God and rescue His most precious creation at the same time.

The intent of this book is not to frustrate and discourage any person or church, but to rally everyone who is saved to recog-nize the urgency and propriety of putting away distractions. How quickly we are moving toward the end of the Church age and the beginning of all eternity. I truly believe that time is of the essence.

ANYONE CAN

"We never do great things without trying."

Reinhard Bonnke

If you were able to take the time to study each aspect of the human body it would astound and amaze you. The human body is so complex and so remarkable in its design and function that medical scientists today are still baffled by its complexities. Additionally, each human body is one of a kind. Each individual human being carries a distinct DNA structure, fingerprint, and even voice pattern. No two of us are the same. So it is in the Body of Christ. There is one body, yet many billions of parts. Each part fits perfectly into an eternally grand design that benefits the Lord in a clearly unique way. God made each of us to be the only "puzzle piece" that will fit in just a certain way, so that when creation steps back to get a better look, surprisingly, the whole puzzle looks just like Jesus. Each one of us is a specific brush stroke in a tapestry intended to bestow honor on its Artist. Wow, what a great idea from the Master Painter!

We should realize, therefore, that we are needed and that we are each vitally significant to God's process of Kingdom advancement. When we realize this, we begin to see God in a new light and our role in a new light. Sometime ago, a well-meaning friend came up to me and with all sincerity said, "AC, God does not need you." As soon as the words were coming out of his mouth I heard another Voice say, "Don't listen to him. I did not send him and he does not speak for Me. I need you, AC, and I created you in order to use you." I never forgot that day. Afterward, I had a spring in my step as my heart leapt for joy! God had spoken deep into my heart in direct rebuttal to the voice of the world. Up to that point I was genuinely struggling with my own self-worth. It is amazing how God can change your entire life with just a sentence— especially after you've heard nothing but negative about yourself all your life.

You see, I grew up never hearing that I was important or special to anyone. I was born to a mother who died when I was just 6 months old and to a father who was put in prison (for all I know). I was tossed about from foster home to foster home as an orphaned baby and landed in a severely abusive foster home at the age of about one or two. In this home I was handed out the cruel combination of physical and emotional torture. Each day I was told by these "foster parents" that I would "amount to nothing in life" and that I was a "retard". This was followed by sadistic physical beatings at night. I well remember being kicked in the head many, many times, and beat with belt buckles on top of my head. Additionally, I remember being punched and slapped repeatedly and other things that may not be appropriate to mention at this time.

I struggled internally to survive as well. As a young child, not only did I have such a cruel home life, but I was also very unpopular and frowned upon by the kids at school. I constantly reverted to a deep well of dark depression, even inventing imaginary worlds where I was important and not abused. This went on for many years until I was nearly fifteen. At that point I left the abusive home to strike out on my own. I figured that the streets were much safer than in the house with the abusive adults. It worked. Within two weeks God had brought me to a wonderful Christian family that lived in the same town. Larry and Dottie Wilson had committed their entire lives to rescuing "nobodies" like me. They had witnessed so many children come and go through their home, and then there stood me. I had no talents, was not liked by anyone in school, looked peculiar, and possibly even smelled up the front foyer of their living room. In other words, I was to be the proverbial "handful". Still, Larry and Dottie took the chance and welcomed me into their home.

That was March of 1981. To this day, though I have a family of my own, the Wilsons are still my true "parents" and we have a wonderful relationship. During the early years living with the Wilsons, they introduced me to the greatest gift ever—Jesus Christ. They demonstrated their love for Him by loving and taking care of me. It paid off! Through much patience and determination they continued to hold up the banner of Christ over my life, even when I displayed mild forms of rebellion and all-out stupidity. They received the news from me in a letter in March of 1988 that I had surrendered my life to Jesus Christ and that I would never be the same again. Since that moment, I have dedicated my life to being a child of God and doing His will. I'll just bet, when they think of me and reflect on their commitment to rescue children, there are tears of joy and satisfaction in their eyes.

The desire in my life since conversion has been to utilize everything for His great purpose of advancing His Gospel. He used each experience—the good, the bad, and the ugly to transform me personally, but most importantly, to help transform others. God does not waste any experience. If we, when we are facing the issues of life, would stop and ask, "Who is this going to benefit, Lord?" we might go through that experience with a different outlook.

Consequently, we should conclude that when God blesses us in this life, He does so in order to bless others. In fact, I strongly believe that God does nothing *for* us that He does not also want to do *through* us.

God deeply loves us all and knows every detail about us. He shaped us a certain way in order to make His glory known through us to those around us. We need to find solace in that and be willing and ready to convey that to as many as possible.

So, where does that bring us today? I believe it whispers to our delicate hearts just how much God needs us. The next time someone tries to convince you otherwise, gently remind them of what our Master said in Matthew 9:37-38:

37 He said to his disciples, "The harvest is great, but the workers are few. 38 So pray to the Lord who is in charge of the harvest; ask him to send more workers into his fields."

God needs workers! He needs people! When is the last time a rock lead someone to Christ? How long has it been since a tree reached out to a hungry child and fed that child a scrumptious and nutritious meal? Can you recall the last time a building stepped off its foundation to go to an unreached people group somewhere in the Congo? How often, if ever, does a laptop computer jump off the desk to visit your neighbor who has just lost his job? It is time for you to discover what I and so many others have discovered, that life is not worth living unless lived out for the Great Plan of God.

Chapter One

We are All Ministers

"If you think you're too small to have an impact, try going to bed with a mosquito in the room."

Anita Roddick

As I pressed forcefully against the back tire of the trailer, I felt a slight movement. Suddenly, I found myself two feet off the ground and into the air! I came down hard with a splat into the thick, mushy Nicaraguan mud. I was covered head to toe and lying face down in the mud. I heard a loud cheer erupt from behind me. My impromptu cheering section was lead by some jubilant missionary team members from Gardendale Baptist Church in Gardendale, Alabama, together with the seasoned IMB missionaries, Jim and Viola Palmer. In unison they laughed as they cheered, "He's one of us now! He's one of us now!"

Unbeknownst to me, I was unceremoniously inducted into the middle of an unintentional initiation moment that seemed par for the course on that particular trip. The work was strenuous and yet the camaraderie was impeccable. We were digging ourselves out of the mud on our return trip from delivering clothes, supplies, and medicine to a very remote village outside of Puerta Cabeza, Nicaragua. The Palmers have an incredible ministry in that area to the Miskito Indian people. We were helping the Palmers with some cleanup efforts in direct response to a terrible hurricane that swept through the area. The Miskito people are subsistence farmers and very poor; the hurricane had wreaked havoc on their already delicate lives.

When the week was over, my body was very sore from the immense construction work, but my heart was overjoyed. The team from Gardendale Baptist Church was lead by my friend, Richard Bradley. This man has taken nearly every spare moment of the last nine years of his life and dedicated that time to travel to Nicaragua to minister to the practical needs of the Miskito Indians. He, along with the vigorously hardworking missionary couple, the Palmers, has solidified a place in my heart as a man of purpose—*a man on a mission.*

It is amazing to note that Richard is not a preacher, yet he has made such an impact in world missions. Richard probably does not get too many offers to be the keynote speaker at conferences; however, this man could easily hold his own conference on the specific needs of an unreached people group. Additionally, he could easily have been the one to write this book. Oh, but I guess he wouldn't because taking the time to sit and write when he could be installing some plumbing for the first time in the home of a family of eight somewhere in a remote village in Nicaragua. That's a true hero in the faith.

The team members from Gardendale, as well as Richard Bradley, realized that we are all called to mission fields. Here's a statement for you to ponder: Each person in the world is either a *missionary* or a *mission field.*

Missionary or Mission Field

Either you are reaching others with the love of Christ or you are in need of reaching yourself. It's just that simple. There are no innocent bystanders in Christ. Neither are there any neutral parties. We are all either engaged in the work of the Lord or we are not a part of Him at all. Reinhard Bonnke, the famous evangelist who has led nearly 100 million people to Christ in this decade alone, once said, "A person who does not reach the lost is lost himself."

Consider carefully the words of our Savior in Luke 11:23:

23"He who is not with me is against me, and he who does not gather with me, scatters." (NIV)

Now, marry the concept from Luke 11:23 with two other passages written in red letters:

Luke 19:10 "For the Son of Man came to seek and save those who are lost." and Mark 6:15 "Go into all the world and preach the Good News to everyone."

It's no secret—Jesus came to accomplish a specific mission and He expects His children to get on board with that mission. At the moment of regeneration the Holy Spirit ingeniously deposits the desire to proclaim the Gospel into the heart of a true believer. True believers are characterized in large part by their uncontrollable desire to share the Good News that they have received. They just can't stop talking about it and about Him. No matter where you come from or what you have experienced, you won't be able to get away from the compelling heart of the Savior as He eggs you on to reach out to lost and hurting people.

That notwithstanding, if you cannot remember the last time you cared enough to reach out to a lost person and tell them about the reason for the hope inside of you, perhaps that "hope" is, in fact, not in you. If we continue to follow this kind of reasoning, we could say that whether or not we are willing to go on mission for God may determine whether we are genuinely God's children or just swimming around in the outer courts of religious observance. We should be able to test the validity of our faith by using this plumb line. (II Corinthians 13:5)

Are you on mission for God yet? If not, why? What is holding you? Have you ever tasted His heavenly Gift? Have you ever offered your life to Christ to serve Him and Him alone? Perhaps you struggle with the fear of man, or perhaps you have been entangled by the control religious inoculation brings.

Challenging the Status Quo and Sacred Cows

Anyone who has grown up in the Church can easily identify with the church culture. The church culture seems to follow
the same pattern as every other culture—it *excludes* and *creates*
barriers. In addition, only those who have adapted well enough to
the cultural conditions are given the privilege to take up perma-
nent residence. In many mainline denominations those barriers are
strong and fortified. Those churches have written and unwritten
rules to govern entry levels for beginners. Additionally, they have
exclusive codes to govern the continuation of status and citizenship
within their culture. "That's just the way we do it" some churches
maintain. "We've never done it that way before" others point out.

Any person who has not grown up in the Church tends to form
a predisposition against the Church based on how the Church has
excluded them culturally. In other words—they all feel left out!
Why? The one culture that is designed to integrate and inspire all
other cultures is actually distancing itself from mainstream society!
This is not due to the *Message* it preaches, nor the *Persona* it
elevates, but because of the *manner* in which it *propagates*. The
Church, by nature, should be the most inviting environment on the
planet; yet it seems to be the least inviting. The Church tends to
display heat instead of light, pomp instead of passion, and control
instead of compassion. How does this happen? It happens when
we embrace *church culture* instead of *Christ culture*. The church
culture says, "Come look, talk, and live like us, and then you can
become one of us!"

Ponder for a moment the following passage from Luke 15:1:

> *"Tax collectors and other notorious sinners often came to*
> *listen to Jesus teach."*

Jesus drew crowds of people from mainstream society, due in
part to His miracles. A portion of this passage also says that "they
came to listen to Him teach." Of course the people responded to
the miracles Jesus performed, but they also clamored to hear Him
speak. He taught within their culture reminding them of a God

Who has always loved them. His words brought hope to them. His life caused them to want to emulate Him and be around Him. Do people want to be around us? Do we push them away because of our righteousness and their conviction, or perhaps because of the way we push our church culture on them instead of simply offering them Christ.

Within the *church culture* there stands the twin support beams of *status quo* and *sacred cows*. By status quo, I mean the way things have always been done. By sacred cow, I mean traditions that are not biblical, yet some churches hold to them anyway.

For a moment, and for the context of this book, let's just examine two:

1.- Specially trained "clergy" are to do the ministry; and
2.- Regular "laity" people are simply to support those "clergy" ministers.

Though there are dozens of passages of scripture we could use to make a strong case against these fallacies in the Church, for now we'll just take four:

Mark 16:15-18

15 And then he told them, "Go into all the world and preach the Good News to everyone. 16 Anyone who believes and is baptized will be saved. But anyone who refuses to believe will be condemned. 17 These miraculous signs will accompany those who believe: They will cast out demons in my name, and they will speak in new languages.[a] 18 They will be able to handle snakes with safety, and if they drink anything poisonous, it won't hurt them. They will be able to place their hands on the sick, and they will be healed."

Notice in verses 17 and 18 that Jesus was very clear that His Message and His Gospel would be advanced by "those who believe." While it is true that Jesus called a select group of men

37

to run the show (leadership), they were not the entire show themselves. He was very clear in His instructions, and we should be very careful not to hinder believers from ministering.

Acts 8:1-7

1 Saul was one of the witnesses, and he agreed completely with the killing of Stephen. A great wave of persecution began that day, sweeping over the church in Jerusalem; and all the believers except the apostles were scattered through the regions of Judea and Samaria. 2 (Some devout men came and buried Stephen with great mourning.) 3 But Saul was going everywhere to destroy the church. He went from house to house, dragging out both men and women to throw them into prison. 4 But the believers who were scattered preached the Good News about Jesus wherever they went. 5 Philip, for example, went to the city of Samaria and told the people there about the Messiah. 6 Crowds listened intently to Philip because they were eager to hear his message and see the miraculous signs he did. 7 Many evil[a] spirits were cast out, screaming as they left their victims. And many who had been paralyzed or lame were healed.

In these passages we clearly see that according to verse 4 "the *believers* who were scattered preached the Good News about Jesus wherever they went." That was everyone! Then in verse 5 we note that Phillip, a food distributor and waiter from Acts 6:5 (one of Stephen's buddies), was used by God in an extraordinary fashion as he preached the eternal Message of salvation.

Ephesians 4:11-12

11 Now these are the gifts Christ gave to the church: the apostles, the prophets, the evangelists, and the pastors and teachers. 12 Their responsibility is to equip God's people to do his work and build up the church, the body of Christ.

From these two powerful passages Paul makes it clear that the "job" of the trained and commissioned leadership of the Church is simple: "Their responsibility is to equip God's people to do His work and build up the Church, the Body of Christ". One glance at some churches today and you might see the opposite. Church leadership has bought into the idea that they are the ones paid by the church to do all the works of the ministry (i.e., visit the sick and those in prison, conduct revival meetings, and preach regularly from the pulpit).

But what are pastors, teachers, apostles, prophets, and evangelists to be doing? They are to be *serving* the saints, *training* the saints, *equipping* the saints, and *sending* the saints. Those are their main functions and duties.

Hebrews 10:24

24 Let us think of ways to motivate one another to acts of love and good works.

Each time we gather together in our churches we should be concentrating much of our time and energy on this verse. We have the opportunity each week (no matter what day or time of the week your church meets) to "spur" one another on to go out and do the work of the ministry.

Perhaps the Church is in a season today when we need some reformers like Martin Luther. We need those passionate God fearers to awaken and stand up against, not the people or leadership of the Church (that's called rebellion), but against those ideas and ideals that keep the people in the Church—just that, "in" the Church.

Putting an End to Missionary Myths

By this point any one of us might be thinking, "Hey, yeah, that's right. I should be the one doing the ministry, not just my pastor!" While this might seem like a positive revelation, be careful that you are not diving off into pride. We are the ones called to do the work of the ministry, yes, but we are to submit to leadership in the process. Additionally, we should recognize that many of us harbor certain stigmas and grapple with certain missionary myths which have built ramparts against our faith. We cannot seem to shake these myths because they are engrained in the minds of our church culture mentality. However, if not dealt with, they can easily block each of us as individual believers from ever stepping out into the mission God has in store for us. Two of the primary missionary myths to which we tend to gravitate are:

1.- It takes a special *call* to go on mission for God; and
2.- It takes a specially *gifted person* to go on mission for God.

Let's deal with the first one— *"It takes a special call to go on mission for God."*

The truth is, as previously mentioned, God has already made just such a call and sent it out to *every* Christian. So, either every Christian is considered special, or the statement is false. You cannot have it both ways if you embrace the passages we mentioned earlier. Each individual Christian is already called to go. Consider another passage of scripture:

Matthew 28:18-19

18 Jesus came and told his disciples, "I have been given all authority in heaven and on earth. 19 Therefore, go and make disciples of all the nations, baptizing them in the name of the Father and the Son and the Holy Spirit.

These passages are commonly referred to as the Great Commission.

What do you think Jesus was saying here? Is it possible that He was being literal—that He sincerely desired that we *all* go to the nations? I believe it is abundantly clear.

I well remember the late Keith Green in his memorial concert video footage passionately proclaiming to the audience, "If you don't hear a call, know this—you are already called (to go)!"

Every believer may not be called to move overseas, but every believer is called to *connect with* and be a part of *completing* the Great Commission.

Ok, now let's look at the second myth— *"It takes a specially gifted person to go on mission for God."*

This myth creates a false sense of pride in those who do answer the call to go and it fosters a sense of apathy in those who don't. We should outright reject the myth and begin to take *what God has given to each of us* and *dedicate* it to God's mission call, and take *how God has made us* and *integrate* it into God's specific plan to fulfill that call.

We are not all the same and yet we are all desperately needed to fulfill the Great Commission. We've already discussed many times in this book the fact that God needs us and desires to use us just the way He made us. In this next chapter, we will unpack that whole concept. I want you to be able to realize to a greater degree your personal value and involvement in the grand scheme of things and begin to strategize concerning the necessary steps needed in order to jump in with both feet.

Chapter Two

For Whom is God Shopping?

*"I am not what I ought to be. I am not what I wish to be. I
am not even what I hope to be.
But by the cross of Christ, I am not what I was."*

John Newton

The stillness of the night was abruptly interrupted by a faint
crackling noise, only to be followed by the frightful sensa-
tion of a massive creature making its way apprehensively across
my forearm. Without hesitation, I frantically slapped the unseen
intruder away from me. I jumped out of bed as quickly as I could
to turn on the light. The sudden noise woke up my wife and
daughter, and they, alarmed, asked me what was happening.

"I think one of our huge spider friends just crawled on my
arm!" I answered.

It didn't take long for all of us to go on a massive search under
the beds and throughout the room looking for the creature. After a
futile thirty minute room-wide inspection, we gave up the hunt. My
wife said, "I'll bet he's halfway to Delhi by now."

As we began our casual descent back into bed ready to put the
whole unwanted sleep intermission behind us (it was 3:00 am),
Victoria, my daughter who had joined the fracas with us, suddenly
pointed to my wife's back and screamed, "There he is!"

I quickly slapped the creature off her back and crushed it. To our surprise, it was a giant black scorpion! The unwelcomed intruder had been in my wife's hair for thirty minutes! My wife's reaction was understandably one of distress. My daughter was amazed and somewhat excited. And me? Well, the first thought that went through my mind was, "Now that's something you could only see in India."

Truly, there are so many things you could only see in India. Our family, in the short six months that we were fortunate enough to live in that beautiful, yet spiritually empty country, witnessed more things than we could ever describe. Most of them were wonderful, and some...well...were kind of creepy.

In that half-year's time the Lord used our family to help lead one hundred and one precious Indian people to Christ, begin a church-planting movement, and help bolster the evangelism strategies and efforts of two sensationally anointed and precious national believers —and all from the confines of our simple little kitchen!

We had dreamed of moving overseas to advance the Gospel to unreached areas ever since we got married. Amy Lynn gave me her hand in marriage one week after I looked into her beautiful eyes in late August 1998 and said, "Amy, marrying me will be going out on a limb." By the "limb" I simply meant that she would be giving up much more than she bargained for since I knew what the station of my life would be to go out to find the *unreached* and *reach* them.

Ten years earlier and just one week after I received Christ in 1988, I applied for my passport. Ministry to the unreached around the world and the destitute around my hometown became priority.

Consequently, since those early remarkable days as a new believer, I have had the privilege of preaching the Gospel in ten different countries and to sixteen different people groups. I got involved early and served through my local church in any ministry where I could fit. Most of the ministry experience I had, however, came by accident. The opportunities came just by seeing a need and filling it. There were always so many people who had desperate spiritual and physical needs. From the inner city street children in my hometown and the desperate hungry people abroad, to the hurting lonely family members in ICU waiting rooms in the local hospital, there was enough to do to fill up my weekly itinerary for nearly ten years.

Because of this I never finished college. I was clearly instructed by the Lord to learn from Him and to walk by faith through doors that He opened. This was tough to do since I witnessed many of my contemporaries receiving their seminary degrees. Following God's leading, however, demonstrated to me over the years of His desire to use "anyone." He just needs "anyone" to be available for His instructions and that they abandon themselves to carryout His cause.

That night in India, though the scorpion freaked us all out, I had to reflect back on years of putting it all on the line in so many different settings. The glories had far outweighed the headaches and the Lord had demolished the remnants of a past littered with the trash of sin, failure, and low self-worth.

Rhodes Scholars, Supermen, and Top Dogs not Required

Acts 4:13

> *"The members of the council were amazed when they saw the boldness of Peter and John, for they could see that they were ordinary men with no special training in the Scriptures. They also recognized them as men who had been with Jesus."*

It is a serious misconception on our part to reduce ministry to the highest common denominator (i.e., the most gifted and well trained). So often we attach more value and place more emphasis on *superstars* than we do on *servants*. We ooh and aah at the talents of those who make their ministry life on stage, and although we probably don't intend to, we celebrate those of *high profile* as though they are *high priority*.

The Church today seems challenged by society to embrace *upward mobility* (the capacity or capability for rising to a higher social or economic position), while Jesus is challenging His

Church to embrace *downward nobility* (a phrase which suggests that we are to celebrate as noble the lowest social or economic denominators). We must resist the continuing temptation to promote the popular, the best, or the most affluent. It may seem to make us all look better, but it doesn't please God and it doesn't get the job done.

We should be preparing our churches to become *sending depots*. This can happen when we recognize that we are not the same in *function*, but we are in *value*. Leaders in churches have a God ordained responsibility to both recognize this way of thinking and to quickly implement it.

Reinhard Bonnke often says, "God is not looking for supermen." He also says that God is looking to be the hero for a large number of zeros. God wants His kingdom advanced, but He needs to be King and to be glorified. It is pure pride and arrogance to suggest otherwise.

Let's take a quick peek at the ministry of Jesus to discover His take on this.

Matthew 9:35-10:16

35 Jesus traveled through all the towns and villages of that area, teaching in the synagogues and announcing the Good News about the Kingdom. And he healed every kind of disease and illness. 36 When he saw the crowds, he had compassion on them because they were confused and helpless, like sheep without a shepherd. 37 He said to his disciples, "The harvest is great, but the workers are few. 38 So pray to the Lord who is in charge of the harvest; ask him to send more workers into his fields."

Matthew 10:1

Jesus called his twelve disciples together and gave them authority to cast out evil spirits and to heal every kind of disease and illness. 2 Here are the names of the twelve apostles: first, Simon (also called Peter), then Andrew

(Peter's brother), James (son of Zebedee), John (James' brother), 3 Philip, Bartholomew, Thomas, Matthew (the tax collector), James (son of Alphaeus), Thaddaeus, 4 Simon (the zealot), Judas Iscariot (who later betrayed him). 5 Jesus sent out the twelve apostles with these instructions: "Don't go to the Gentiles or the Samaritans, 6 but only to the people of Israel—God's lost sheep. 7 Go and announce to them that the Kingdom of Heaven is near. 8 Heal the sick, raise the dead, cure those with leprosy, and cast out demons. Give as freely as you have received! 9 "Don't take any money in your money belts—no gold, silver, or even copper coins. 10 Don't carry a traveler's bag with a change of clothes and sandals or even a walking stick. Don't hesitate to accept hospitality, because those who work deserve to be fed. 11 "Whenever you enter a city or village, search for a worthy person and stay in his home until you leave town. 12 When you enter the home, give it your blessing. 13 If it turns out to be a worthy home, let your blessing stand; if it is not, take back the blessing. 14 If any household or town refuses to welcome you or listen to your message, shake its dust from your feet as you leave. 15 I tell you the truth, the wicked cities of Sodom and Gomorrah will be better off than such a town on the judgment day. 16 "Look, I am sending you out as sheep among wolves. So be as shrewd as snakes and harmless as doves.

What an amazingly revolutionary section in our Bibles! Now, let's dissect it for a moment:

Notice Jesus' mission.

9:35-36 - Jesus was out preaching, healing, and ministering in remarkable ways. He understood His mission to the letter and performed it without fail.

Notice Jesus' passion and urgency.

9:37-38 - Jesus candidly appealed to the ones that were kind of following behind Him to see what He saw—a large harvest ready to be won and a small group of workers ready to do it.

Notice *who* He recruited.

10:2-4 - What a motley crew! Have you ever stopped to think about just *who* Jesus chose for His disciples? Let's look at some on His list:

1.- Illiterate, probably drunken, fishermen: Simon and Andrew
2.- Hot headed, overly ambitious brothers: James and John
3.- A wishy-washy doubter: Thomas
4.- A despised tax collector: Matthew
5.- An insurgent: Simon the Zealot
6.- A backstabbing betrayer: Judas

Notice, as well, that none of them had proven themselves in any way to be loyal, trustworthy, or in any way "excellent." They weren't trained, qualified, or specially gifted. They weren't even endorsed! It may be, as well, that they weren't well-liked by those in the synagogue, nor their village, and perhaps not even in their own families. As far as we know, the only license they had for ministry was a fishing license.

Most public relation types in churches today would gasp and ask, "What was He thinking?"

Notice what He did *for* them.

10:1 - He gave them extraordinary authority and power. Wow, even before they were tested! Jesus staked His authority on these for whom most churches would throw away.

Notice what He expected *from* them.

10:5-20 - Jesus did not hold back because these men were untested or unqualified. He gave them His power and authority and sent them out with clear, detailed instructions. He expected miraculous results as well. Today, has He changed His mind and His methods since times have changed? The answer is absolutely not! We have changed, He has not. Just because many church leaders don't obey Him and do things His way, doesn't mean that He does it theirs.

Do you see how far we have come? Do you see how "off the mark" many church leaders have been who took enthusiastic and innocent believers and squashed their gifts and threw the water of religion on their fire? What a shame! Why do we have to take new believers and sit them down for years to observe whether or not they will make the grade? Why do we wait for years to endorse hungry, passionate missionaries? Why are we so afraid to place hands on people and commission them? Why do we feel so compelled to send a microscopic number of people off to be trained when we have hundreds of already surrendered and faithful people chomping at the bit to be significant for God right down on the first five rows of any given church? What will Jesus say to us leaders who ascribe to that? Will He say, "Well done" when we have refused to obey Him and shut up the kingdom of heaven against the "least of these"?

Jesus turned the world upside down with this "motley crew" and today it seems as though, in all our eagerness for excellence, we are trying to turn the world back again — back to self-centered, high-profiled religion that stifles and suffocates.

But we must not forget that Jesus is still in charge of His Church.

He has a very important mission, and He is not going first to the universities to find His leaders for this mission, but to the streets and shorelines of any town or village in the world. He will not allow His Holy Spirit to be upstaged by "great training facilities" nor "great programs and systems." He must be honored, glorified, and obeyed. Nothing else counts.

The Difference between Commissioning and Ordaining

God loves His Church and chooses to use His local churches in each community to drastically impact the spiritual, economic, and social horizon of any region. The Church should be a local recruiting station and sending depot for all the new recruits (believers) awaiting their turn to be deployed into the Great War for souls.

I'll never forget a sermon I heard way back in 1989 by Pastor Tommy Barnett. The title of the sermon was "It's in the House." Pastor Barnett gave one of the most stirring sermons ever on the value of those sitting in the pew to the great call of God for the Great Harvest. He suggested that church leaders look no further than to the people who served day in and day out in their churches in order to launch out in every direction and into every nation. I strongly believe that some churches would begin looking to implement this revolutionary idea if they understood the importance of the definition of two specific terms—*commissioning* and *ordaining*.

Commissioning is the laying on of hands by local church leaders (sometimes in the form of a presbytery) for the purpose of sending those commissioned to specific mission work outside the confines of the church. We find this term (or concept) primarily in the New Testament. It's certain that most people have heard of the Great Commission, but many have never heard of the concept of *commissioning* as it applies to the local church.

A classic example of this is found in Acts 13:1-4, and it gives a wonderful illustration of the blueprint of a local church as mentioned in the section, *The State of Things.*

The church leaders in Antioch heard a definite command from the Holy Spirit to separate two men and commission them. They sent them out to spread the Gospel. What might have happened in many churches today if they were given the same command? Would they respond the same way? Would they even be ready to do so? Might they be tempted to hoard their congregants, namely their "best" leaders?

Local churches should be willing to send every willing participant, especially their best. So many times "gifted" people are offered the opportunity to parade their gifts on the stages of our churches, but not in the trenches of world missions where they might get the supreme return and reward.

Local churches could easily discontinue their regularly scheduled "discipleship" programs and instead begin implementing regular "commissioning courses' for their people, training and equipping as many people as possible with the slogan, "We do not want to be known for our seating capacity, but our sending capacity."

Ordaining is also the laying on of hands by local church leaders, but is primarily for the purpose of special functions within the Church and for the sake of those already inside the Church. This practice is best illustrated in I Timothy 3:1-13 and Titus 1:5-9 where Paul gives specific instructions for appointing elders, overseers, and deacons to ministry of the Body of Christ within the Church. In the context of appointing leaders (ordaining), the process should not be rushed, but given much consideration. In other words, it's about training the chiefs, not the Indians, and it's for ruling within the teepee.

The largest portion of the Body of Christ, however, is not represented by ordaining, and therefore the need for commissioning. Why? Because the task of fulfilling the Great Commission will not happen by the leaders, but by the workers.

Replacing Self-Esteem with God-Esteem

So often I hear people contend that the reason they don't step out for God is because they feel inadequate. They often reflect what their peers in society have said about them; comments such as, "I'm just not good enough" or "I will never amount to anything." If you hear those things enough, you start to believe them. Like our contemporary society today many churches foster environments of exclusiveness and isolation. We isolate those within the Body of Christ who are not like us. We promote the ideal that our churches are families and are for every person, yet act as if only the socially elite can thrive within.

Just as I mentioned earlier about the Church culture and the restrictions that apply, such is the condition of many mainline churches. You often hear it from those outside the church (which we would do well to listen) as they sarcastically assert that "the Church is nothing more than a social club."

So, how can believers ever step out in faith toward the mission field on behalf of the local church if they are not endorsed by or encouraged by the local church? How can believers even attempt to get on board with God's dream to be used by Him when the "headquarters" from where they are commanded to launch refuses to even acknowledge them or their value?

If you are reading this now and find yourself saying "amen" because you have personally experienced this, my encouragement to you today is for you to wholeheartedly replace the idea of boosting your *self-esteem* with the idea of embracing *God-esteem*.

Self-esteem suggests looking *inside yourself* in order to find worth. What you think of yourself and what others think of you determines your value. Tragically, the Church today, much like the world today, places value on people by their net worth or their contributing worth, forgetting, of course, the teachings of Jesus and of James 2:1-9

God-esteem, on the other hand, suggests *looking up* to the *Person of Jesus* to find your worth. What He says about you and thinks of you is what determines your value. A beautiful example of this is found in the passages in Luke 12:4-7.

Could you imagine never having to worry again what people think about you? Wouldn't it be awesome to be able to wake up every morning knowing that you are loved and accepted by the most influential and popular Being in all the universe? What would your ministry life look like if you were able to remember daily that the King has sent you on a special and significant mission, so it doesn't really matter what His subjects think of you or your mission?

Committing today to living with God-esteem will open up a door of freedom and confidence that will bring abundant life to you and eternal life for many through you. Get on board now, don't waste time. Don't live anymore for the approval of people. Don't wait until you feel good enough about yourself, because your King needs you and the world awaits you.

Don't Forget Personal Holiness (I Peter 1:13-16)

Holiness is not perfection. It is, however, a state of thinking, speaking, and living as close to what Jesus Christ did while He was on the earth as possible.

God desires to use each one of us and will if we let Him, yet He won't compromise holiness. He is holy and perfect and wishes to be represented for exactly who He is. He wants each of us who carry His name and proclaim His Message to do so in the purest and most holy fashion. He doesn't let down His standards and He knows that without holiness no one will ever experience Him or taste heaven. (Hebrews 12:14) He desires to reflect Himself to the lost masses and can only do that through "reflect able" (holy) vessels. (Isaiah 52:11)

Let's ponder some important points about holiness from Jesus Himself in Mark 7 as we examine this important issue.

Holiness should be defined by Jesus, not by us. (Mark 7:1-13)

The biggest problem with the Pharisees whom Jesus encountered while on the earth was that they had invented and propagated their own brand of holiness. They had left the purity of the Law of Moses by adding their own rules and decisively diluting any emphasis God had originally intended. In doing this they had shut out both God and man. They were a nasty bunch of rulers who did their best to have the Lord of Glory crucified—and all while thinking that they were impressing God and doing His will.

Allow the Lord's Spirit and His Word to define your convictions and you will both please Him and be useful to Him.

Holiness works from the inside out. (Mark 7:14-23)

At the root of religion stands the intrinsic matter of true holiness and where it should start. The dark and sinister evil of legalism emphasizes an outward appearance of holiness instead of an inward change. Jesus denounced this kind of holiness as both faulty and faithless. He pointed out to the Pharisees that they were substituting God's sacred Word for their own traditions. This kind of "holiness" has caused the eternal demise of millions throughout history.

God's true holiness has nothing to do with how we look on the outside. His holiness works from the inside out. He cleans us up and miraculously transforms our hearts (or affections) and our minds (or attention) and blazes a completely straight path for our feet (our ambition and agenda). He is the One who does the filling and the freeing, the cleaning and the comforting, the anointing and the appointing. We will discuss much more in detail on this in the next chapter, *Anointed and Appointed.*

Holiness should be attractive and convicting. (Mark 7:24-26)

If you've ever met a true believer (the born-again kind), you see how incredibly attractive yet convicting they can be. In fact, most of them do so without ever saying a word. Their very lives are billboards to God's amazing and wonderful grace. They have a sense of true holiness that speaks volumes, yet many times they come under the social radar because they don't readily announce their holiness. Here's a short list of the very attractive characteristics of true believers. They are:

1.- Happy, enthusiastic, and encouraging

True happiness comes from true holiness. When a believer is connected to the one true Source of holiness that believer does not strive as much. They seem to care so much more about others and they embrace the idea that each day they live is a golden opportunity to encourage someone or lead someone to Christ.

2.- *Humble, yet confident*

True holiness will humble you, yet build your confidence at the same time. Why? Because you tend to remember from where holiness comes—the Lord. Additionally, you tend to rely more heavily on His holiness than your own. This causes you to live life above all circumstances and despite troubles.

3.- *Faithful and comfortable*

Those who are holy are automatically faithful, yet they don't make people feel uncomfortable in being so. In other words, they are supremely loyal to their own personal convictions, while allowing others sublime freedom. They hate their own sin and focus on their personal deliverance so that they can untie the knots of others' lives. They don't freak out and they don't control people because they don't need anyone to control.

4.- *Heavenly minded and earthly good*

When a person is truly holy, their minds are frequently on the things of eternity. Therefore, they are more susceptible to being productive here on earth. They have already cashed in on their allegiance to the world to come and live here only to pick up as many pieces as they can before they go.

Living with holiness is to be desired as you step out to reach out. Your mission from God on this earth will always include holiness. We will dissect this much greater in the section *Sanctify While You Testify* in the second chapter of Section Two **Everyone Must**. Stay tuned.

Chapter Three

Anointed and Appointed

*"The wind of the Holy Spirit is not sent to cool us down
but to fan the flame."*

Reinhard Bonnke

The large truck inched gradually through the pothole filled path surrounded by mounds of debris. The stench of trash and raw sewage were blended conspicuously with billows of smoke which rose persistently as if to lay a blanket over the sky. The sights of families huddled under makeshift lean-tos amidst the heaps of garbage offered a glaring glimpse of the reality that was staring back at me. Standing in the back of the truck and straddling five gallon gas cans and supply boxes, I braced myself against the constant battering from being tossed around in the back of the truck, then readied myself for the upcoming task. With one hand I covered my mouth to shield both the smells and the winds that whipped up indiscriminately against my face, and with the other hand I carefully cradled a small snack and drink. The refreshments were to be handed down to the people rummaging through the dense mounds of trash there in the middle of the Guatemala City Dump.

I glanced over the truck rail in time to notice one particularly dirty young boy sifting frantically through the garbage. He seemed to have discovered a half-eaten sandwich and was beginning to put the sandwich toward his mouth. I couldn't believe my eyes! He was eating a revolting morsel right out of the trash and didn't seem to care! He spotted our relief truck and quickly abandoned his trash-filled turf to secure a spot closer to us. As he approached the truck, I peered into his eyes like a detective looking for clues in an attempt to extract any vestige of hope from his gaze. His eyes stared back at me with yearning, but no hope. He reached gratefully up for the snack, and then turned quickly to face back toward the direction of a small tin-roofed refuge amongst the refuse.

I felt so inadequate to offer any real help. I was frustrated and even felt somewhat ashamed. The simple snack I was giving out couldn't possibly even make a dent in his hunger, and I seriously doubted that he or anyone here in this dump would even listen to me if I were to tell them about God's great love for them. How would they ever get to know Him? They live in trash! They survive from others' discards. I remember thinking, "How can I reach them, Lord?" Visible results would have to wait for the moment since I had a task of feeding hungry people and couldn't afford to stop.

Later that night, just before I went to sleep, however, I prayed fervently and asked the Lord to use the simple outreach from the day in the dump to transform a community of historically suffering people. God met with me in those moments to convince me that even simple service to hurting people, when engineered by and anointed by the Holy Spirit, can make a miraculous difference. There was mission work in my future that would impact the world and God was showing me the most expedient and productive way to make it happen. Much like a refreshing shower after a mud bath I felt exhilarated and reassured. It convinced me, as never before, to rely on the power and leading of the Holy Spirit in all of my mission outreach efforts, even those that seem to be the most futile.

The Purpose and Role of the Holy Spirit in Missions

God is the infinite and matchlessly powerful God who is committed to sending His Message of Hope to a lost world; and He knows exactly how to do it!

He does it all through the Third Person of the Trinity, the Holy Spirit. Everything in missions and in the Church is designed by the Lord to be inspired, inaugurated, and enhanced by the Person of the Holy Spirit. He is to be the One who brings power and purpose to all of our preaching efforts. He is the One who brings the fire of evangelism and the fulfillment of the Great Commission. He is the invisible yet very viable One who encourages, convicts, and creates life in the midst of a dead, cold world.

We must realize that when focusing on missions, the Holy Spirit has come to both *anoint* us with His power and *appoint* us to a special task decreed by His authority.

Anoint means to apply oil to consecrate someone who has been chosen for a specific, divinely inspired ministry. The Holy Spirit is that "oil" applied to us setting us apart to accomplish the mission God has purposed for us. He seeks to place His seal of ownership and proprietorship on all those who truly believe in Jesus and who are willing to submit to His leadership.

His anointing carries divine:
    Authority;
    Authenticity; and
    Approval

His anointing manifests in:
    Miracles;
    Purity; and
    Favor

Appoint means to fix or set officially for specific missions. We, as true believers, are appointed by God to go to every person everywhere and preach the Gospel to them. We need not ask whether or not we should go, but instead, how is it that we are to go. We should be ready and willing to go anywhere, anytime for the sake of Christ.

What did Jesus say about the Holy Spirit?

Our Master made some very clear assertions concerning the Holy Spirit, especially in conjunction with the propagation of

His Gospel. John chapters 15 and 16 give us insight, as do key passages in Luke 24:47-49, and Acts 1:4-8.

The Holy Spirit points everyone and everything to the Person of Jesus Christ.

John 15:26-27; 16:15

26 But I will send you the Advocate – the Spirit of Truth. He will come to you from the Father and will testify all about Me. 27 And you must also testify about Me because you have been with Me from the beginning of My ministry.

15 All that belongs to the Father is Mine. This is why I said, 'The Spirit will tell you whatever He receives from Me.'"

Understanding the significance and purpose of the Holy Spirit does not have to be complicated because Jesus made it abundantly clear – the Spirit would put all emphasis on Him and get His marching orders from Jesus. And why not? The Holy Spirit is not in competition for acclaim, but ever lives to glorify the Savior and His cause.

Jesus completed the first part of the Mission and the Holy Spirit is set to finish it.

John 16:5-7

5 But now I am going away to the One who sent Me, and not one of you is asking where I am going. 6 Instead, you grieve because of what I've told you. 7 But in fact, it is best for you that I go away, because if I don't, the Advocate won't come. If I do go away, then I will send Him to you.

Jesus basically stated in these verses that unless He left the scene, the rest of the Mission could not go on; namely, the worldwide saturation of the Gospel through the Holy Spirit. Jesus performed many incredible miracles while on the earth. In addition, He taught ageless truths that both revolutionized a generation and brought a radical shift to the future ideals of mankind. He exemplified perfection in every way and was the single most compassionate, caring, and sacrificial person of all time. His work of redemption for human beings was flawless and ingenious. He proved His true identity and deity in all that He did, leaving no stone unturned or law requirement unfulfilled. His part of the Mission was to come and die for the sins of all humanity, then back to His status in heaven as King and Judge of the universe. Jesus fulfilled His very important part of this Mission to perfection, but all was not finished 40 days after Calvary. There was one more Piece to the puzzle coming right around the bend.

The Holy Spirit would bring perpetual conviction to sinners.

John 16:8

And when He comes, He will convict the world of its sin, and of God's righteousness, and of the coming judgment.

Part of the ingenious plan for salvation was the duel need of softening up the hard heart and conveying the righteous standard of the Holy God to lost people. Without this duel-purpose component in place, many people would never turn to Christ for salvation. First of all, they would never know that they were provoking God's wrath, shaming themselves, or even doing anything wrong, without someone to bring shame to their heart and convince them of their need for a Savior. The Holy Spirit is the One who does just that. In the Old Covenant the written code (the Law) served this purpose. Jesus then came and fulfilled the requirements and expectations of the Law, and then released every bit of the job of convicting into the hands of the Holy Spirit.

Jesus wants us to rely on the power of the Holy Spirit completely as we embark.

Luke 24:47-49

47 It was also written that this Message would be proclaimed in the authority of His name to all the nations, beginning in Jerusalem, and there is forgiveness of sins for all who repent. 48 You are witnesses of all these things. 49 And now I will send the Holy Spirit, just as My Father promised. But stay here in the city until the Holy Spirit comes and fills you with power from Heaven.

Acts 1:4-8

4 Once when He was eating with them, He commanded them, "Do not leave Jerusalem until the Father sends you the Gift He promised, as I told you before. 5 John baptized with water, but in just a few days you will be baptized with the Holy Spirit." 6 So when the apostles were with Jesus, they kept asking Him, "Lord has the time come for you to free Israel and restore the kingdom?" 7 He replied, "The Father alone has the authority to set those dates and times, and they are not for you to know. 8 But you will receive power when the Holy Spirit comes upon you. And you will be My witnesses, telling people about Me everywhere – in Jerusalem, throughout Judea, in Samaria, and to the ends of the earth."

Have you ever tried to drive your car on fumes? Have you ever tried to do strenuous work without eating? Have you ever tried to sail without hoisting the sails? Have you ever tried to make it through a 24-hour day without breathing? Most of us would laugh at these questions because they seem absurd. However, much more absurd is our attempting to live for Christ or minister His Gospel without the power of the Holy Spirit. Many believers rely heavily on education, training, skills, or even willpower. However, without the power of the Holy Spirit, according to Jesus, we are wasting our time. Jesus' desire is that we intimately know His Holy Spirit and rely on Him for everything.

Jesus put enormous emphasis on the Holy Spirit. Additionally, Jesus rarely mentioned nor alluded to the word or concept of *water baptism* (Mark 16:16, John 4:2), but did place distinction several times on the *baptism of the Holy Spirit.* (Mark 1:8, Luke 3:16, Acts 1:5) We should not diminish the importance of water baptism, but simply give more attention to the baptism of fire (the Holy Spirit). Incredibly, today, many mainline churches place most of their emphasis on water baptism and none on the baptism of the Holy Spirit. Could this be one reason why there is so little power and excitement today in many mainline churches and in the Body of Christ as a whole in America? We have left the Holy Spirit high and dry, opting to promote only the things we can understand with our cognitive reasoning. We have shut the door in the face of the Spirit by embracing programs and systems over Him. This is a tragedy of eternal proportions!

So, what should we do? What should our immediate response be today in order to make this right?

Our Response Needed

There are different camps of thought on the Holy Spirit and, even at times, a volatile divergence over the subject of the baptism of the Holy Spirit. Some contend that the Spirit is given without measure at the point of salvation. (Ephesians 1:13-14) Others, however, maintain a theological position which says that the Holy Spirit is a separate experience which occurs after salvation. (Acts 2:1-4, 38; 8:14-17; 19:1-7) Either way, the Holy Spirit does not come on the scene to divide Christ's Body, but to *edify, intensify, electrify,* and *solidify* it. He is not to be used as a theological weapon against other members of the Body at all. In fact, I think that kind of stuff makes Him a little mad, and we do not want to grieve the Holy Spirit. (Ephesians 4:30). So, here are some points to ponder concerning our role in response to the Holy Spirit.

We need to ask Him for His power for effective evangelism.

Luke 24:49; Acts 1:5, 2:1-5

To reiterate, according to Jesus, we are to wait on the Holy Spirit in order to get the power that we need. And believe me, we need power! We cannot do what we are expected to do in order to fulfill the Great Commission without power from above. Why? Because we are not strong; we are not omnipresent; we are not able to change the souls of men. But, when we commit to obtaining His power first, the results of our efforts are greatly augmented and we see immediate, lasting, supernatural fruit.

We need to ask Him to fill us constantly.

Luke 3:16,22; John 3:34; Acts 2:17-18, 4:8,31, 7:55;

Romans 8:10-11; Ephesians 5:18-19

Under the Old Covenant men and women of God, at rare times, had the Holy Spirit come "upon" them for special ministry. Under the New Covenant, however, the Holy Spirit is made available to fill up the individual believer and church with His presence as much as that individual believer and church desires to be filled. The purpose of His "filling" is to bring joy, strength, and purity. We cannot get these without His constant presence.

We need to be controlled by the Holy Spirit in our personal lives.

Romans 8:5-9; Galatians 5:16-26; I Thessalonians 5:23-24

Those believers who exemplify victory over sin in their lives would tell you, if given half a chance, the only way that they are able to do so is because they allow the Holy Spirit to control them and not the other way around. We must be ready to not only be filled with the Spirit every day, but controlled by Him all during the day. When He is in control, we are not. He controls us from the inside out, changing our "want-to" and causing us to fulfill His will.

We need to fully rely on Him for guidance.

Luke 12:12; John 14:26, 16:13; Acts 13:1-3

The Holy Spirit knows what is best for our lives and for His mission. He needs to be in charge of the ambitions and agendas of our lives. We should not just fill up our day timers with busyness, but be "on-line" with the Spirit of God to get His take on our regularly scheduled lives. We benefit greatly from this, as do the people whose lives we touch, because we are surrendered to the Holy Spirit's guidance. Additionally, He won't lead us into snake pits. Yes, there will be times we will venture, by the leading of the Holy Spirit, into challenges which are miles above our ability to conquer, but the Holy Spirit will give us Himself to make up the difference and bring us to the other side.

We need to be careful not to resist, grieve, or blaspheme the Holy Spirit.

Luke 12:10; Acts 5:1-11; I Thessalonians 5:19; Hebrews 10:29

Before we think that the Holy Spirit is our "Great Errand Boy," ready at our ever beckoning call, we must remember that He is every bit God and is not to be trifled with, nor shunned, nor neglected. We are actually the ones who are to be at His ever beckoning call. We are to be His "errand boys," ready to wait on Him hand and foot. He is holy and perfect, and, though He is a gentle giant, He comes, nevertheless, to take charge. There are so many in mainline church circles who treat Him as if He were not important, spurning His love and rejecting His authority. Where do you think so called "believers" like that will end up? Those who trample Him by pursuing programs, principles, and systems above Him, then speak against those through whom He is manifesting, await a doom far more dark and gloomy than those who never believed. This should be a stern warning to all of us, especially those of us who are in leadership or are teachers. We will have a greater condemnation, so let us humble ourselves and exclusively seek His face, His involvement, and His leadership.

The world awaits missionaries who are sold out to the cause of Christ, but more importantly, filled with the Holy Spirit, because they are the ones who make the most dramatic and lasting impact. You can and should be that missionary. God can make you become everything He desires you to become. Chase the presence of the Holy Spirit and embrace Him for all He is and for all He brings into your life. Don't leave home without Him.

The call is ringing out to a new generation of sold out soldiers who refuse to allow the popular vote to keep them from abounding in their task. He is also upgrading the tempo of world harvest and pushing millions of missionaries out to gather that harvest in before the end. That end is coming soon, and that door of opportunity is closing. It's time to get into the game before it's over. Anyone can, now everyone must!

EVERYONE MUST

*"We talk of the Second Coming; half of the world has
never heard of the first."*

Oswald J. Smith

Imagine for a moment that the world is just like a super highway
containing eight lanes for traffic. The first 7 lanes to the left are
designated for vehicles speeding along at no less than 150 miles
per hour. The remaining lane farthest to the right is the slow lane
for travelers cruising along at 100 miles per hour.

Every driver on this super highway seems consumed with
getting somewhere (anywhere) as fast as possible. Suddenly, you
look up ahead and on the horizon you notice that there is a huge
breach in the pavement. The road abruptly drops off creating a
horrifying cliff just miles ahead. You notice hundreds of cars plum-
meting off this sudden ravine and you are stunned with genuine
terror at the sight. You hear the screams of those falling into the
chasm and notice the sheer horror on their faces.

Seconds later, however, you notice an exit ramp mere yards
away from the horrific drop off, and it leads up and away from
the disaster. Spontaneous hope rises inside you and a real sense
of urgency emerges. With the exit ramp in sight you take off in
desperation toward the speeding traffic to warn as many drivers
as possible of the unexpected tragedy. You have one thing on your
mind—get them to the exit ramp.

Nothing else matters to you at that point. You aren't worried if your clothes are in style or if your hair is straight. You aren't thinking about your 401k plan or your excellent portfolio. Not once do you think about your latest golf score or the latest kill mounted on your wall from your local taxidermist.

You are not the least bit concerned if the people on the highway know you or not, or if they will be offended by your warnings and hysterical pleas. You have not questioned if you are qualified for this new vocation and are not apprehensive as to whether or not you have been given permission or endorsement by anyone in charge. You simply rush unthinkingly toward the drop off to warn those in traffic of the doom that awaits them.

This is the point to which your heart beats faster and faster, tears are prevalent, and your voice gets hoarse quickly. You've sprinted past the point of no return without a thought except to warn, to rescue, to save.

Or...you stand there and do nothing.

You see, this illustration is directly related to the reality of missions. Countless numbers of people are racing toward eternity unaware of the consequences ahead of them. On the other hand, it may be that they just haven't been told about the eternal chasm up ahead. They need to know. They need to have someone get their attention and rescue them before it is too late.

That's why this book was written. I believe that a wakeup call needs to be given to the Church at large to rally and appeal for laborers. I am writing the book, but in reality I am holding up a sign before all who will take notice.

Chapter One

No Parking Here

*"Some wish to live within the sound of a chapel bell, I wish
to run a rescue mission a yard from hell."*

C.T. Studd

The door flung open and the wave of people came rushing toward me shouting and wildly clutching my arms. This same wave started pushing me backwards until I felt like I would be trampled. I lifted my head above the crowd for a second and noticed a man standing next to a vehicle parked mere yards away. He was motioning with his hand and yelling instructions over the noise of the crowd. I thought for a split second, "Now how in the world am I to get to this guy?" I could barely see him and I was starting to even lose oxygen. I knew somehow, though, that this guy was my only way of escape from this hoard of people that were about to crush me.

Finally, with one last ditch effort, I pulled myself up, grabbed my two bags, and began pushing against the crowd like a fullback in football trying to hit the gap on a goal line stand. In fact, that was the image in my head as I put my head down and hoped for the best. Suddenly, I saw a ray of sunshine through a small hole in the crowd and I shot the gap with reckless abandon. I managed to get through just as the man standing at the vehicle extended his hand toward me to pull me the rest of the way to his car. He was the missionary I had come to visit in the city of Port Au Prince, Haiti. There was a hint of concern on his face, which turned quickly to a huge smile, as he said, "Welcome to Haiti. Good job keeping your head down and coming away with your bags intact. Now, let's go!"

I hastily threw my bags into the back and promptly jumped into the same space of the vehicle with the bags. The only way I could ride was to lay on top of the bags with my foot lodged deep into a small crevice on the floorboard. We rode for nearly two hours over pothole-filled streets. I could barely see out from the mound of luggage, but I could make out some of the landscape of Haiti. Immediately my heart began racing with fear and contempt as I witnessed open, running sewage with children playing in and around the sewage. I saw the pitiful Haitian houses made of one piece of rusted tin and two sticks crudely accommodating four or five people bunched uncomfortably together.

I was twenty-four years old and had only been outside the states into Mexico before this trip. Those first moments in Haiti quickly gave me a reality check regarding missions. I couldn't turn back! I was stuck in a country that, by first impressions, was freaking me out, to say the least. Then, as if venturing into a different world all together, I began to remember the commitment I had made to Christ just two years earlier. I recalled, in those few seconds, how much I had fallen in love with Jesus, and how wonderful He had been to me every moment of my new life in Him. I courageously blurted out in those cramped quarters of the vehicle that day rolling precariously down the city streets of Port Au Prince, Haiti, "Jesus, You are worth it!"

I knew that I would never be the same again, and that the call of God on my life would take me places I could never imagine, many of which I may not enjoy. I knew, however, that my love for Christ could not be lived out in neutral. I would have to pick my two feet up and get moving and never stop.

God is Looking for Laborers

Matthew 9:35-38

Anyone who reads these words of Jesus should be able to clearly identify the expression of the Master's heart for missions, and equally be able to conclude that the "laborers" He was referring to must be His followers—that's us! As Jesus was traveling throughout the towns and villages, no doubt He saw the overwhelming needs and was upholding the standard of His original purpose which He expressed in Luke 19:10, "For the Son of Man came to seek and to save those who are lost." He never deviated from that purpose, all the way to the agonizing death on the cross.

Recently I spent ten unforgettable days in Ethiopia. For three of those days our small team ministered in remote villages surrounding the capital city of Addis Abeba. We spent two nights sleeping in churches made of mud and cow manure and surrounded by fields of wheat and teth. Much like in the Holy Land of Israel, agricultural elements of the Bible seem to come to life in Ethiopia. The above passages in Matthew came alive to me while I served in these villages. Since our team was there during harvest time, I noticed that in these villages the harvest seemed to mean everything to these poor farmers. Every member of the family was industriously aiding in the gathering of the harvest. Entire families, including small children, were out in the fields working hard to meet their quota for survival. I thought, "Why can't the Body of Christ see the harvest of souls around the world in this way?" I also thought about the sentiments of Jesus as He lived on the earth and called out to all who would listen to join in collecting His harvest.

Two thousand years later this same proclamation is going out to all believers. Earlier we discussed that He is not looking for only special people to hire, but for all of His followers. Those who answer the Lord's call receive benefits both during their lifetime and into eternity. As a preacher once said concerning ministry, "Hey, the pay isn't great, but the retirement benefits are out of this world!"

Now, let's look at these laborers for Christ. There are certain noticeable characteristics about them that clearly set them apart. Laborers for Christ:

Understand, love, and are devoted to their assignment.

True laborers have a keen sense of destiny and purpose. They know that there is nothing more important than the task of seeking out and reaching those who are lost. Though there is much in life to distract them, these laborers are married to the cause of Christ; they literally exist for that purpose, and they seem to just love it!

Utilize their God-given skills to accomplish their assignment.

Laborers for Christ have *discovered* the gifts that God has given them, but more importantly, they have *dedicated* those gifts for the purpose of bringing in the harvest. They know that utilizing what God has given them to accomplish His dream gives them great fulfillment and satisfaction.

Chase after their CEO's approval.

There's a phrase so often used today that says, "Living for the audience of one." These Christ-laborers don't use this phrase for pious rhetoric, they live it! They have not only received Christ as their Savior, but their Boss as well. They realize that He is the CEO of the universe and is the highest and greatest prize for their lifetime of labor. They quickly chase away any agenda or ambition that has not been sent as a memo from their Awesome Employer. May their tribe increase!

If you have received Christ as your Savior, you now have the opportunity to let Him control every ambition and pursuit of your life. He is worth it.

God is Enlisting People of Action

When I was a little boy, I watched the weekly TV series *Batman*. In the late 60s version of the Dark Knight, there was always a cheesy fight scene between Batman and Robin and some evil henchmen. What I remember, besides the terribly choreographed fight scenes, was the cartoon captions that always popped up when Batman or Robin would slug one of the bad guys. The captions made the fight fun—kapow, pop, smack, blammo—and made me run off and punch walls to simulate the sounds just like the action hero.

Today, in our churches and in our lives, we need a good dose of kapow, pop, smack, and blammo! In other words, we need some real action. What we tend to drift toward in our busy church schedules is not always *action*, but many times just *activity*. We tend to "go through the motions" year after agonizingly mediocre year. If we have a system in place, we tend to stick with it no matter the results. We lean on so many programs designed for evangelism, yet recruit so few fiery evangelists. Then, when the programs don't net harvest-like results, we spiritualize it by resigning, "I guess it's just not God's timing," or "Well, guess we need to leave the results in the Lord's hands." We blame our ineffective cerebral evangelism results on the Lord of the harvest! From heaven, meanwhile, He is blaming it on us!

It reminds me of what I heard David Shibley say, "It's like rearranging the furniture while the house is on fire."

We should take note of this, repent, and start beseeching the Lord of the harvest to send us and others in our church toward lost people or bust! We should cut loose any programs or systems that don't help bring in the harvest.

Consider the Gospel itself, what it was meant for, and how it was supposed to be propagated. David Livingstone, the great pioneer missionary to Africa during the 1800s said, "The end of the geographical sphere is only the beginning of the missionary enterprise."

1.- The Gospel is always moving forward
2.- The Gospel is always pushing on borders
3.- The Gospel is always running through open doors

The Lord is enlisting men and women of action to keep up with His demands for the Gospel. He needs some action heroes of today. Let's look at some ways we can become those action heroes:

Pray for the power and fire of the Holy Spirit.

As discussed earlier, Jesus puts tremendous emphasis on the need for the power and fire of the Holy Spirit for evangelization. Luke 24:49 says, "And now I will send the Holy Spirit, just as My Father promised. But stay here in the city until the Holy Spirit comes and fills you with power from Heaven." Also in Acts 1:4-5 Jesus commands, "Do not leave Jerusalem until the Father sends you the Gift He promised, as I told you before John baptized with water, but in just a few days you will be baptized with the Holy Spirit."

The Holy Spirit brings life and supernatural action to our lives and ministries (Romans 8:11—one of my favorite passages); there-fore, we need to pray for His presence and power to overcome our inabilities and insufficiencies at evangelization. In other words, we cannot do it without Him.

Be content with everything except evangelism results.

The Lord is proud of us when we display thankful and content hearts about everything in our lives except one—evangelism results. God desires a fire and an ambition for souls that keeps us on the cutting edge and on the edge of our seats with anticipation. He wants us to ask Him for the nations (Psalm 2:8) and then tena-ciously pursue evangelization of those nations.

Commit to adapting to the different ways God wants to move.

Those who refuse to get bogged down in traditions or methods that have proven to fail commit themselves instead to make any necessary adjustments that keep them on God's page. They realize that God cannot be put into boxes made by man and that He wants His children to be sensitive to the cultures they are pursuing, the seasons they are in, and the move of His Spirit as He leads out into the harvest.

Each One Reach Thousands

In many discipleship programs today there is a catchy phrase used, "Each one reach one." I completely understand this philosophy of discipleship and it sounds real nice, yet think about it—what would a farmer look like if he went out to reap the harvest and simply brought back one stalk of wheat? Smiling, and with acres of wheat behind him going to waste, he might sheepishly say, "I got this one."

Or, what would a mom look like returning home from shopping with just one of her four kids? Would she say, "Well, it was worth it for this one." What would you think of her?

Let's also do the math here. Missiological census takers today roughly maintain that there are nearly 1.2 billion Christians in the world today. Meanwhile, world population records state that there are just over 6.5 billion people living in the world. Using the logic of "each one reach one" only 2.4 billion people would be reached for Christ. That's only one-third of the population! I honestly can't see God getting excited about those numbers?

The reality of those numbers makes the case even more absurd. In truth, of the 1.2 billion recorded believers in the world, a large number of those may simply be "nominal" (in name only) Christians, and many are not evangelical. That number is reduced greatly when you understand that even in "evangelical" churches many Christians struggle tremendously with evangelizing a single person per year. So, a conservative estimate might make the number of true evangelical believers closer to 800-900 million. If that is the case (and we are assuming that it might be), then numbers of those reached through the "each one reach one" philosophy makes world evangelization nothing more than a drop in a bucket.

Reinhard Bonnke is quoted as saying, "I don't believe that after Satan has been put into his eternal hellish abode he should be able to say to God, 'You may have gotten me, but I have more than You!'" Bonnke goes on to say, "I make it my aim, every time I have a microphone in my hand, to empty hell and populate heaven!"

Someone asked me recently, "How do we know how many people we are destined to win to Christ?" I quickly replied, "Well, how many do you want to win?" You see, instead of "each one reach one," I propose "each one try to win thousands!" Does that mean we will each accomplish that? I believe we can. I believe, along with Bonnke, that God desires to win to heaven much more than the devil wins to hell. Whether or not it happens, I personally believe, is up to the Church.

Chapter Two

Getting Over Into the Fast Lane

"In the vast plain of the north I have sometimes seen,
in the morning sun,
the smoke of a thousand villages where no missionary
has ever been."

Robert Moffat

W e drove through the busy and narrow streets at a high rate
of speed, nearly hitting three unsuspecting pedestrians who
seemed completely oblivious to anything out of the ordinary. I
------ several times, let out a yelp, and was even tempted to make
to slow down. Without warning, the
turn tossing me from the far left of
el of the far right. My head hit with
ough, and sat up straight trying to
k like I was hurt, and certainly didn't
red. My pride was rising along-
ined to demonstrate to those in the
andle maniacal missionary driving.
y back at me, offered me a seemingly
briefly just in time to cut another
a parking lot. The car came to such a
ked forward into the front seat.

77

Impervious to my personal demise, the driver asked, "You ok?" and then quickly instructed, "Great, come on, we don't have a second to lose!" I had been riding through the streets of Bia Mare, Romania with the pastor of Biruinta Church, Daniel Cherije. He was a spiritual giant in the area and his church was instrumental in making a huge difference in the lives of many in and around Bia Mare. Although his driving had scared me witless, there was a sense of calm in his demeanor that reassured me through the ordeal that it was probable that we just might live through it. After all, he was a pastor, and I was his special guest. How often do you hear of pastors killing or maiming their special guests while driving them to an event? A few minutes passed before I was calm enough to settle into a brisk walk up the steps toward the television studio we were visiting.

Pastor Daniel was hurrying to get to the Romania national television network studios in time to present the Gospel to his hometown of Bia Mare. He told me just as we were ascending the steps toward the studio that I was going to preach on television. "You have to be ready at any time and in any situation to preach with your whole heart this Gospel." Daniel encouraged. And so, off we went to do just that! Daniel frequently preached from this television studio because he knew it was the most expeditious way to share the Gospel. He was ready, and he expected me to be as well.

This short, stocky, olive skinned, dark haired pastor had a personality that made everyone love him, yet a tenacity that made everyone respect him. Daniel Cherije was the kind of man whose passion made you wince from shame at being even remotely lazy, though he never tried to do so. Every aspect of his life echoed an ardent pursuit of hurting and lost Romanians. Though he suffered pain and discomfort from kidney ailments to the point of having to go on dialysis, this stalwart man of God never complained nor let up. His congregation was constantly full and well represented by two genres of Romanians, the young motivated "new generation" and the older generation only two decades removed from communism and terrible suffering.

The few days I spent with Pastor Daniel and his congregation, caused incontestable veneration toward the Romanian people.

They sang worship songs from their hearts, not with their mouths. I couldn't help but stand and admire the older women in the babushkas, knowing that some had witnessed their husbands and sons murdered or tortured by the Romanian secret police. And this day at the television studio was a lesson for me to be aware of redeeming every given moment for the cause of evangelism. I realized that my life was in motion toward evangelism, but I just needed to push down the gas pedal a little, and make a fervent run toward the lost, just like Pastor Daniel Cherije.

I might drive a little less assertive through the city streets in my hometown, but my heart is nonetheless racing toward lost people at top notch speed. Thanks to men of God like Daniel, I realize that time is vital and souls are at stake. I can't embrace personal safety while people are perishing. I can't slow down because I'm tired or sick. I can't allow speed bumps of sin and worry to weigh me down. I must kick it into high gear and go for it!

Discovering the Urgency of God

John 9:4

"We must quickly carry out the tasks assigned us by the One who sent us. The night is coming, and then no one can work."

God is in a hurry! Though many might question the theological validity of that statement, I find it hard to think any other way. Since we know that He does not want anyone to perish, but all to have eternal life in Him, we have to realize that He is more serious about getting His Gospel out than anything else. His tempo for accomplishing this is upgrading in every generation. Every time a person perishes it both breaks His heart and makes Him rush that much more to deploy messengers of His Good News to the remaining lost people.

Luke 14:16-21

*16 Jesus replied with this story: "A man prepared a great feast and sent out many invitations. 17 When the banquet was ready, he sent his servant to tell the guests, 'Come, the banquet is ready.' 18 But they all began making excuses. One said, 'I have just bought a field and must inspect it. Please excuse me.' 19 Another said, 'I have just bought five pairs of oxen, and I want to try them out. Please excuse me.' 20 Another said, 'I now have a wife, so I can't come.' 21 The servant returned and told his master what they had said. His master was furious and said, 'Go **quickly** into the streets and alleys of the town and invite the poor, the crippled, the blind, and the lame.' 22 After the servant had done this, he reported, 'There is still room for more.' 23 So his master said, 'Go out into the country lanes and behind the hedges and urge anyone you find to come, so that the house will be full. 24 For none of those I first invited will get even the smallest taste of my banquet.'"*

Notice the word "quickly" Jesus uses in the parable is the same as He uses in John 9:4. He is expressing the heart of God for people everywhere, especially the overlooked and overburdened, to receive His invitation for that eternal banquet.

God is not some kind of cosmic "watcher" who refuses involvement in the affairs of mankind. He is also not an uncaring parent who easily shrugs off losing a few million children to His arch enemy. He is constantly trying to get His "saved ones" to reach out to "lost ones" and do so with a major sense of urgency. God is the ultimate "First Responder" in the epic struggle for eternal souls.

Consider this scene in a restaurant: A man is eating at a table next to you and suddenly begins to choke on a piece of steak. He becomes desperate as his breathing becomes constricted, and moves from table to table seeking help from the other patrons. As he clutches his throat and silently waves his hands, there is no mistaking that this man is choking and in serious trouble. It is obvious that his life is hanging in the balance and every second counts. But, to his horror, everyone in the restaurant turns away from him, as if to say, "Hey, he's the one who doesn't know how to chew a perfectly good steak. It's not my fault and it's not my problem. After all, I can breathe fine. I'm not choking. Anyway, what if I do get involved and nothing happens?"

What would the man think at that moment? Would he really care who took the time to get involved and give him the Heimlich Maneuver? Would he get mad if that person was not of his race or gender? Would he care one bit whether or not that person was popular, rich, or even cool? No! He just wants to breathe! He just wants to live! Time is crucial in that scenario as it is in the world of evangelism and missions. Lost souls are dying and crying out for someone, anyone, to respond quickly and stretch out their hands to pull them out of the clutches of death.

Consider, also, that a packaging and delivery company called FedEx has more urgency to get their customers' packages to them on time than we do in sharing the Gospel. The Lord spoke to my wife and me as we prepared to return home from India that we would one day impact the entire world with the Gospel. He spoke to my heart the motto of FedEx, "When the Gospel absolutely, positively has to be there overnight" to encourage us to do so expediently. I believe God was saying, "AC, why should a packaging company get their product overseas overnight and My Church does not do the same?" That is all I needed, and now I am dedicated to that motto for my own life—get to the lost now!

Consider, as well, that the devil also has a sense of urgency. We see this clearly in the world today. There has been a rise in mass killings and wickedness has never before been seen such a large scale. Satan is trying to take out as many as he can before the Gospel can take root. In the last century the world became very familiar with the terms "genocide" and "ethnic cleansing." In fact, in that century, though incredible numbers of people received Christ through huge Gospel crusades (Billy Graham, Reinhard Bonnke, Luis Palau, and others), many more were murdered in cold blood under the watchful eye of the international community. It has seemed that, as miraculous as the Gospel crusades have been lately (Bonnke in Nigeria), they simply cannot keep up with the number of lost people being killed before they can be reached for God.

A little history lesson will reveal that although the world claimed there would never be another holocaust, there have been countless examples of genocide. This has proven the theory that the only thing we haven't learned from history is that we haven't learned from history. For example, directly following World War II, it was discovered that the Russian leader Joseph Stalin had been "purging" his country of anyone who opposed his communistic regime. Before he was finished, Stalin had outdone his German contemporary Hitler by slaughtering over 15 million Russian people.

Just thirty years later, the world stood aghast at the barbaric murders of hundreds of thousands of Cambodian people under Pol Pot and the Khmer Rouge. In the 90s there was the Bosnian butcher of Serbs, the mass killing of the Kurds by Saddam Hussein in Iraq, and the 100-day genocide in Rwanda in which nearly a million Tutsi people were systematically murdered in the dirt streets by the Hutus.

It hasn't stopped there. Since the beginning of the 21st century, we are witnessing genocide and ethnic cleansing in Darfur, Sudan. Nearly 400,000 people have perished since 2003 in the western part of Sudan, and the killings and atrocities continue.

Why is it that Satan has a sense of urgency, yet so many churches do not? It is as though we are conceding defeat. We are forfeiting the victory that Jesus handed to us by handing it right back to the devil. His tenacity at killing as many as he can over-arches our willingness and obedience to get out and save as many as we can.

Thankfully, when it comes to the sanctification process of each of us who believe, God is patient and slow to get uptight. He handles our petty issues with gentleness and understanding. However, when it comes to a soul perishing without Him, God is not patient, understanding, nor content. He cannot be. He created those people for His good pleasure. He made them to be with Him forever and performed the greatest sacrificial act by giving up Himself for them.

II Corinthians 6:1-2

"1 As God's partners we beg you not to accept this marvelous gift of god's kindness and then ignore it. 2 For God says, 'At just the right time, I heard you. On the day of salvation, I helped you.' Indeed, the 'right time' is now. Today is the day of salvation."

There are more ways to discover God's urgency than just taking my word for it. Here are some points to ponder:

Take a week to fast and pray.

There's no magic to fasting and the act itself does not change you, the Lord changes you. However, when you fast and pray, you are accomplishing two powerful things:

1.- Giving all your attention to the Lord; and
2.- Saying to your flesh, "You are not in charge."

During that week, ask the Lord to draw you to His heart.

The Lord will draw near to you when you draw near to Him, and He will be looking to draw you not just to His will but His heart. Good earthly fathers don't just ask their children to come sit on their laps to give their children instruction, but also attention, affection, and to share the father's heart.

When He begins to show you His deep burdens, listen.

Any good conversation has talking and listening by both parties. If one only talks and does not listen, it is not conversation, and neither, with God, is it prayer. When we draw near to the Lord, we come to experience love, grace, and instruction. We do ourselves and many a favor when we learn to listen to the Lord and be ready to respond. When we genuinely seek, not only God's will for our lives, but His heart for the world, we will come away with His sense of urgency.

But, there are still some personal hurdles that we must be ready to overcome.

Don't Wait for the Perfect Scenario

Though so many of us agree that we need to get out into the world and preach the Gospel, just as many of us are waiting until all the planets are aligned. It appears that many of us are hoping for that perfect scenario. Some of us are waiting "until the kids are grown," or "if mom and dad get behind us," or something else. There's always the financial aspect of our lives that tends to put restraints on us. We often think, "One day, when I'm out of debt, I'll find out what God wants me to do." We also feel we should have a nest egg in place to provide for our future. We just want to make sure everything is safe and secure before we step out on faith; however, that is no faith at all.

Luke 9:57-60

57 As they were walking along, someone said to Jesus, "I will follow you wherever you go." 58 But Jesus replied, "Foxes have dens to live in, and birds have nests, but the Son of Man has no place even to lay his head." 59 He said to another person, "Come, follow me." The man agreed, but he said, "Lord, first let me return home and bury my father." 60 But Jesus told him, "Let the spiritually dead bury their own dead![a] Your duty is to go and preach about the Kingdom of God." 61 Another said, "Yes, Lord, I will follow you, but first let me say good-bye to my family." 62 But Jesus told him, "Anyone who puts a hand to the plow and then looks back is not fit for the Kingdom of God."

New Testament believers were radical in their thinking and in their lifestyles. They just did not care for their own lives, indeed, even unto death. They were sold out and married to Jesus and His cause. Today, in many developing or oppressed nations, you find the same kind of mindset. Believers in China, for example, are ready to die to spread the Message of the Gospel, and so many of them do. Believers in India and the Middle East are surrendering their freedom and even their lives for the sake of the Gospel. When told that they are allowed to believe in Jesus as long as they do not spread His Message, these believers promptly reply as Peter and John did in Acts 4:18-20 and spread His Gospel everywhere they go. What an amazing way to live!

> *18 "So they called the apostles back in and commanded them never again to speak or teach in the name of Jesus. 19 But Peter and John replied, 'Do you think God wants us to obey you rather than Him? 20 We cannot stop telling about everything we have seen and heard.'"*

In August of 2004, I was sitting in my backyard enjoying a good dose of sunshine and relaxation. My wife and I had been talking for months about planning to move overseas as missionaries. We had met earlier in the year with the recruiter of an outstanding church-planting mission agency and had told him that we would get back in touch with him "someday." I knew that God had called us to go to regions where the Gospel had never taken root, and it was now just a matter of getting our "ducks in a row" and watching all the pieces fall into place. I vividly remember thinking while enjoying the moment, "God, one day we will make our move."

Suddenly, I received a divine rebuttal, as the Lord said, "What are you waiting for?" "Why are you not in a hurry to get there?"

Instantly burdened by a weight of heavy conviction, I knew what the answers were. I had been a spiritual jerk. I had been living my life waiting on things to line up perfectly. I had been an uncaring hypocrite and had been much more concerned for my own comfort and safety than for the souls of those around the world, though I knew better. I quickly jumped out of my comfy chair and hit the ground on my face and knees. I repented right there with tears and renewed compassion. I prayed for the Lord to give me another chance. That day, after confessing my sins to God and to my wife, we called the recruiter from the church-planting agency and started the process toward orientation. We weren't going to waste another day. The rest became, as we say, history.

Here were some of the things plaguing me then, and, I believe, may plague many in the church:

I was trying to maintain a level of comfort.

Comfort is not a bad thing. After all, II Corinthians 1:3-4 tells us that God is interested in our comfort and is the One who can truly bring it. However, when the *pursuit* of comfort keeps us from obeying His call, then His kingdom advancement suffers and His heart is broken.

I was trying to maintain a certain lifestyle.

I found myself caught in a deep rut that I called "my lifestyle." The truth is, I could feel such inadequacy and boredom when I found the lifestyle that I thought I wanted. My lifestyle had very few challenges because I had set it up that way. My lifestyle fostered a lack of compassion and an apathetic mindset that I knew was harming me and others in the long run. I likened it to eating only junk food and sitting around getting obese.

I was trying to maintain social acceptance.

I have always struggled with being concerned with what others thought about me. How foolish to have lived so many years trying to fit into a society that hates Jesus, knowing all the while that I fit into Him just perfectly. If I trade His love and acceptance for the counterfeit the world offers, the result will always be immense sadness and depression.

One day, when all of history is flushed out and ready for judgment, what we do for eternity will be all that stands. Will we wish that we had not waited for everything to fit into our convenience? I'll just bet we will. I know that I don't want to find out.

In the meantime, we have millions upon millions of lives beyond the walls of our comfort and convenience who need to be rescued. Our Heavenly Father is issuing a desperate "Amber Alert" to find His lost children all around the world. Let's get involved. What about now?

Issuing the Amber Alert

It's every family and community's nightmare—a missing child. One minute all is well and the social atmosphere is serene and peaceful, and in just seconds the scene becomes frantic. A child is discovered to be missing and everyone in the community begins scrambling and panicking trying to find this missing child. Local authorities send out what's called an "Amber Alert." This is an alarm signaled throughout the outlying communities that puts the entire region on notice in order to find the child.

All resources are dedicated to finding this lost child. Policemen, firemen, social services, and even private investigators are thrust exclusively into the search and rescue operation. Their single goal is to find the child.

God, through His Church, is trying to do the same thing today. He is utilizing the prophetic voice of the Church to stir up the masses of pew dwellers and Sunday soakers to shout one thing, "Go find my lost children!"

The lost children are all around us, within our very grasp, underneath the shadows of our steeples. They are crying out to the Church to find them, if the Church will only hear and be willing to join the massive search.

Luke 15:3-7

3 Jesus told them this story, 4 "If a man has a hundred sheep and one of them gets lost, what will he do? Won't he

*leave the 99 others in the wilderness and go and search
for the one that is lost until he finds it? 5 And when he
has found it, he will joyfully carry it home on his shoulders. 6 When he arrives, he will call together his friends
and neighbors, saying, 'Rejoice with me because I have
found my lost sheep.' 7 In the same way, there is more joy
in Heaven over one lost sinner who repents and returns
to God than over 99 others who are righteous and haven't
strayed away."*

Jesus is basically saying that the pursuit of lost souls needs to
be the primary and paramount agenda of the Church. Although
ministering to the 99 righteous ones (the ones already saved and
in the Church) is definitely an important aspect of the Church, the
number one focus is clearly to reach lost soul. God continues to
shout, "Emergency, emergency, My children are missing!"

What we do in those first moments after hearing that divine
alarm can make all the difference. Will we hesitate? Will we walk
away with our heads down and our eyes looking away? Or, will
every emotional and devotional fiber of our being snap to attention
ready to answer the call and get wholeheartedly involved in the
great rescue mission?

Imagine if you and your family decided to go the mall for
shopping. You arrive at the mall at 4:00 in the afternoon with the
express purpose of shopping until dinner time at 6:00. You are
meeting with some friends at 6:00 at a restaurant. Around 5:50 you
discover that one of your four children is missing. You last saw the
child mere seconds ago. Suddenly, the rush of emotion and adrena-
line shoots through your head and heart and you begin frantically
searching for your child. Now, its 6:00 and your child has not been
located. Are you worried about being late for the dinner date with
your friends? Are you concerned with finishing your shopping?
Are you saying to yourselves, "Oh well, guess we'll have to go on
without her." Absolutely not!

As it gets later and your child is still missing, your mind is
inundated with thoughts. Every question and every answer that
your mind is processing is based on your love for your child. Then,

as you glance around, you spot a man with a walkie-talkie near his mouth rushing toward you. Your child has been found! Your reaction will more than likely be less than dignified; you will not be concerned about being in control of your emotions. The joy that consumes you at that moment rivals that of the shepherd finding his sheep.

In Luke 15 notice the progression throughout the chapter about "things that are lost." It begins with a lost sheep, moves to a lost coin, and ends appropriately with a lost child. Possibly the clearest unveiling of God's heart for the world can be found in this wonderful chapter, primarily the story of the prodigal son. This story demonstrates what is on the mind and agenda of our great God. He is completely absorbed in His one passion—finding His lost children.

God is not at all careful in His deliberations when it comes to His agenda. He doesn't readily give His stamp of approval on every agenda our churches endorse, especially those that don't involve getting His eternal message of hope and salvation to those who don't yet have it. He is out to find His lost children and He despises it when we won't help.

Isaiah 43:5-6

5 Do not be afraid, for I am with you. I will gather you and your children from east and west. 6 I will say to the north and south, "Bring my sons and daughters back to Israel from the distant corners of the earth."

Chapter Three

Keeping it Simple and on Target

"The ABC of faith is that as we act, God acts."

Reinhard Bonnke

The atmosphere was electrifying as a large crowd began to gather like ants toward our flatbed truck. The people began coming from every corner of the region as soon as they heard the music. Our band was mounted precariously on the narrow flat surface of the truck, presenting quite a challenge to keep in tune and keep from falling off at the same time! We had assembled a team of musicians and preacher-wannabes from the states intent solely on ushering in God's presence for an unforgettable week of Gospel crusades right on the streets of Rio de Janeiro, Brazil. As the people continued to gather, my heart began to race as I was told by our leader that I was first up to preach.

"What?!?" I said. "But I didn't...I mean...I couldn't 'um..."

No time to waste, I was up and I had to preach with thunder and clarity because this was our one shot at this group of people. I turned nervously toward the leader, Phillip Murdoch, a ruddy complexioned missionary with a great passion for people. He had lived for years in Brazil, yet spoke with a thick, Australian accent. Nonsensically, I said, "What should I preach on?" Phillip looked at me with utter surprise; then, seeing both the humor of the moment and the opportunity for a life-lesson, he replied, "Oh, just preach John 10:10 and they'll all get saved."

The only problem with that was I felt like I should "really" preach, and that passage was just too simple and elementary. I guess, due to my prideful heart, I believed I was a true Gospel crusade preacher and being in a rotation of simple people made me feel less important. Additionally, I resented that someone should burst my bubble by reducing my preaching to something so common and ordinary.

Within seconds, however, I had repented of this pride, recovered my wits about me, and jumped up onto the flat bed truck. There it was, the moment of truth. I had to get a message to the expecting crowd that would impact them tremendously. As Phillip had suggested, I began to quote John 10:10. I looked down at him and noticed an obligatory grin on his face, which didn't help my confidence in the least. As I began to preach I realized that the microphone stand was perched at the very edge of the truck. I actually had only an inch of space to work with and had to continually look down to keep from falling. In addition, the band was so tightly cramped together behind me, that when they moved even slightly, it caused me to tip further toward the edge. The band members seemed oblivious to my situation.

Miraculously, after preaching for a brief five minutes, more than one hundred men, women, and children responded to my simple presentation of the Gospel. I had told them that the devil (the thief) had been trying to steal their joy, kill their families, and destroy their souls for years, but Jesus had come that night to bring them abundant life in Him. This simple message touched their hearts and made them realize their need for an abundant Savior, Jesus Christ. What a wonderful response!

After the crowds cleared and began walking joyfully back toward their houses, I glanced momentarily at Phillip Murdoch. He looked at me as if to say, "Hey man, you got it right, you kept it simple, and God showed out. Way to go. Come back anytime."

I remember that night well because the Lord not only taught me a great lesson, but used me mightily at the same time. I decided then that I would never make the Gospel complicated and I would never stop preaching the Gospel just because I don't have this life completely figured out. I took a lesson from the playbook of a passionate missionary from Brazil, "Keep it simple, but keep it coming."

Understanding the Seasons

I'd like to remind us of an often forgotten foundational principle in Christianity today. That principle cant best be termed as *seedtime and harvest*, but not the way many have used it.

Ecclesiastes 3:1-2

1 For everything there is a season, a time for every activity under Heaven. 2 A time to be born and a time to die, a time to plant and a time to harvest.

This principle is witnessed in nature and in history. It needs to also be in effect in the Church. By that statement, I mean the Church needs to recognize its history as well as what is unfolding in the season it is in today. Why is this important? Primarily because God is up to something and He demonstrates that "something" through seasons of blessing and revelation to and through His Church. God desires to utilize His Church to make the greatest impact possible within the generation it finds itself. God is up to something *special* and *specific* in each generation; something that He wants to *reveal* to *revive*, *impart* to *implant*, and *deposit* to *deploy*.

The Church, which has been around for 2,000 years, has had multiple opportunities throughout the centuries to be an integral part of answering each generation's deepest questions and solving its greatest dilemmas. History records whether the Church accomplished this or squandered it. The times the Church squandered its influence can be traced to many factors, not the least of which is from not knowing its place in history and culture. In the seasons that the Church has not identified nor adapted to that season, the next generation has had to suffer greatly.

Listen to the rebuke that Jesus hands out in Luke 12:54-56:

54 Then Jesus turned to the crowd and said, "When you see clouds beginning to form in the west you say, 'Here comes a shower.' And you are right. 55 When the south wind blows, you say, 'Today will be a scorcher.' And it is. 56 You fools! You know how to interpret the weather signs of the earth and sky, but you don't know how to interpret the present times."

Obviously, Jesus was referring to the religious people who had become experts in conditions around them, but were oblivious to the true identity of the One speaking that day. I believe Jesus continues to say, "Don't miss your opportunity to really know Me, while becoming experts in everything else!"

Understanding Our Season - Point #1

This is not the season for becoming theological experts,
but experts at reaping the harvest.

You might ask, to what are we becoming experts? Sadly, today in many mainline denominations, we are missing our visitation of revival from Jesus because we are so concerned with becoming experts in knowledge, especially *theology*. Without trying to convolute this whole matter, please allow me to give further explanation.

There is a rush to fill our heads with so many things about God that we, like our Pharisaical predecessors, are missing the Savior. The signs of this are obvious as we examine the poisonous divisions in the Body of Christ, all based on a person or group's interpretation of a theological distinctive.

We have become experts in dividing and destroying, not helping and healing. We fight with bitterness and exclusivity and stand over our victims quoting Scripture. We even think we are doing God a favor. The truth is we are making Him angry and judgment is about to be the "season" for many who love theological knowledge above Jesus Himself.

Amos 6:1-4

1 What sorrow awaits you who lounge in luxury in Jerusalem, and you who feel secure in Samaria! You are famous and popular in Israel, and people go to you for help. 2 But go over to Calneh and see what happened there. Then go to the great city of Hamath and down to the city of Gath. You are no better than they were, and look how they were destroyed. 3 You push away every thought of coming disaster, but your actions only bring the day of judgment closer. 4 How terrible for you who sprawl on ivory beds and lounge around on your couches, eating the meat of tender lambs from the flock and of choice calves fattened in the stall.

This is a direct indictment against people who love to "sprawl on ivory beds and lounge around on couches" of theology. In other words, they love to sit around and talk about God, but never get out and do anything for Him!

Now, mind you, theology is good and we need it. After all, we need to believe the truth about God and His Kingdom and Gospel. However, without the motive of love and the action of sharing that love with hurting, loveless people, theology can be binding. (I Corinthians 13:1-2)

A couple of great examples of this are illustrated in the lives of my dear friends at Indigenous Outreach International (IOI). The director, Patrick Beard, and his assistant, Stephen Kennedy, are two of the greatest men I have ever met. They study with passion "to show themselves approved to God." They don't lie back on their theological haunches, simply waiting to share this truth to those who may ask. They "go" living this truth, and they live it to the max! These men are incredible missionaries to Ethiopia, Germany, Ireland, and Brazil; living to fulfill the Great Commission. Patrick is a true "theologian" in every sense of the word. He enjoys talking endlessly about biblical theology, but his passion is to reach lost people, bringing them into relationship with the One who is the object of his studies.

Have you ever given much thought to what issues bring division among many "theologians"? I find that it's not Christian essentials, but non-essentials; such as, some representing that there are contradictions in the Bible. These "contradictions" are not at all contradictions, but points of the overall character of God being expressed through His word. A perfect example of this is the theological position of "election" (Romans 8:29-30; all of Romans 9; Ephesians 1:5, 11; II Peter 1:10) being reconciled with passages in the Bible that state God's heart to see "everyone" in Heaven. (Ezekiel 33:10-11, John 3:16, Romans 10:13, I Timothy 2:3-4, and II Peter 3:9) These don't become contradictions when we, the Church, embrace God's overall character and intent. It's then that we begin to discover that God is not contradicting at all, but is revealing the mysteries of His will. I admit I struggle many times reconciling verses that seem to contradict, but I trust what I have come to "know" about the Lord and never just what I "think" about things.

Understanding Our Season - Point #2

This is the season to become multi-cultural, multi-ethnic, and ecumenical.

Those who hear clearly the voice of the Lord recognize how often He puts emphasis on bringing His Body back together for one final harvest-reaping push. As mentioned earlier in the book, the Church is challenged greatly by an unhealthy dose of fragmentation, and this fragmentation is crippling Kingdom advancement. The number one way to bring in the largest harvest of souls possible and bring the greatest honor to the Lord at the same time is through *ecumenicalism.*

Just think about the impact of churches coming together in an unprecedented manner vigilantly agreeing on one thing: sending out the most romantic message in all of history—God wants to be with humanity forever; and accomplished in the most romantic fashion ever—the demonstration of intimate love for one another. What love! What compassion! What intimacy and wonderful humility! These actions would do astounding damage to the kingdom of darkness and advance the Kingdom of Christ tremendously. Why? Because a great majority of the world has been looking for love in all the wrong places, and the Church has been hoarding it all in one place. Churches could easily reverse this and begin to make an impact immediately if leaders of major mainline denominations would agree to stop fighting and fussing over non-essential aspects of Christianity and move forward *together* with the most essential aspect of all—Jesus is Savior and lost people need Him.

There are many churches today where the light has dawned, and they are making a genuine attempt to implement this among other churches. These churches are committing themselves to the Great Commission in their communities and around the world. They are doing so by building solid bridges of fellowship with other Christian churches. One such church is The Life Church of Memphis and is lead by my friend, John Seibeling. Under John's leadership this body of believers has grown impressively; not only in numerical size within their congregation, but in influence throughout both the churched and unchurched communities. The Life Church is one of the best examples I have seen recently of a multi-ethnic, multi-cultural, and ecumenical church. Nearly half of the congregants and leadership is comprised of minority ethnic groups. The Life Church is recognized as a non-denominational church; however, the fact that nearly all of the mainline denominations are represented, in reality the church is inter-denominational. Praise God! What a church! Sounds like a place most saved people would love to call home and most lost people would love to find.

Understanding Our Season - Point #3

This is not a season to plant seeds, but to reap a great harvest.

When I run into people today who don't seem to demonstrate a hunger for winning souls, I frequently hear them say, "But I'm planting a lot of seeds." I understand that some of them may be genuinely called to do just that, but I truly believe it's much fewer people than we'd think, based on what we see. Millions of souls are perishing around the world at an unbelievable rate, and the Church seems oblivious. Perhaps, instead, it is that the Church is overwhelmed by such doomsday numbers and cannot ready itself in time, or that it simply refuses to believe that the Church is responsible for clearing up this mess.

As mentioned earlier, we must believe that God wants everyone in Heaven and that He wants and needs to use us to get them there. Additionally, we must believe and recognize that Heaven and hell are real and time is running out! We cannot waste another day. God is upgrading His tempo for world harvest, and we must be able to discern that and get on board.

Belief systems play a heavy part in what people do. If someone believes that God is fine with them simply doing the bare minimum in advancing His kingdom, then their actions will prove such a belief. However, if someone believes that God wants everyone to go to Heaven and that He wants and needs to use each believer to get the lost people into Heaven, there will result a harvest of souls produced through those who act on such a belief. They exhibit a passion and a hunger for God's hand to be on them in a direct attempt to pull perishing millions out of the fire of hell.

Missionaries Tim Scott and Will Dekker are two men who exemplify this in every way. These two young missionaries have trekked around the world in search of lost people, and more specifically, unreached people. Unreached people are those who have either never heard or have little or no access to the Gospel. Tim and Will began traveling around the world in 1999. They decided to go anywhere the Spirit of God lead them (much like Paul and Barnabas), especially in search of lost people groups. Their travels have taken them to tiny villages in Africa and India, through dense jungles in Laos and Thailand, to remote Buddhist temples, the frontlines of battle in Afghanistan, and the farthest reaches of the freezing Gobi desert in Mongolia. They have endured thousands of leeches, inedible food, endless and exhausting travel, life-threat-ening blizzards, border patrol hassles, and many sleepless nights, all in pursuit of finding and preaching to those who haven't heard of Jesus. They documented each journey in a reality television series called *Travel the Road.* As Tim and Will venture to new hori-zons each episode, they come across entire tribes of people who have never heard the Gospel, and their frustrating question remains the same, "Jesus died for everyone, so why has no one told you?"

Tim and Will are just two who have heard and answered the clarion call to go on mission. No doubt there are many more like them, but not nearly enough. There are countless millions of believers who haven't yet understood their season in history and their duty to enlist. They, like all of us, must understand that today is the season of great harvest and God needs laborers.

Let me site an example of this which might better illustrate my point. When we moved to India, we had been told that we might not see many converts because the area where we were going to live was just not ready for the Gospel. We were told to go and simply sow seeds and hope for God to water those seeds over time. The problem, however, was that we believed God wanted to do more than that through us. I read the story of William Carey who is considered to be the "Father of Modern Day Missions." William Carey showed up in India in the late 1700s and had the toughest time leading anyone to Christ. In fact, it was seven years before Carey even saw a convert. Carey sacrificed so much in order to bring the Gospel to this spiritually dark Hindu country.

During that same time, there was great upheaval between the colonies in America and Carey's home country of Britain, as the United States of America was declaring its independence from Great Britain. It is strange that simultaneously, Britain was tightening its grip on India as well. There William Carey was, caught in the middle of an international political conflict while trying to pioneer a spiritual path into the vast oppressed nation of India. Equally perplexing was the fact that it was many of Carey's constituents from his beloved England who were crying out in America for freedom from England, while many of his other constituents in England were oppressing the country of India more forcefully each year. As Carey stared at the fabled shores of India, he must have thought about the irony and the hypocrisy of his situation. Additionally, he had to recognize his unique position in history as he began to advance the Gospel into India.

Early in his ministry in India, it became obvious that Carey's pioneering work was to plant seeds of the Gospel deep into the soil of Mother India. Who knows, but possibly he thought, "If I plant deeply, someone will reap the harvest in the generations to come." And...there we were.

Irony often works two ways. It just so happened that we came to live in an area in northern India in the state of Utteranchal, and the house where we lived, get this, was built the very same year that William Carey died. With such history behind us, the Word of God in our mouths, and Heaven supporting our efforts, we just believed that, for the time we were to live in India, we would not plant any more seeds over the ones Carey (and many, many others after Carey) planted. We were going to commit to harvest the souls ready from all that planting!

We just knew that if we had been the ones who planted, we would not appreciate losing that future harvest to someone who is convinced that they should do more planting. It was time to harvest and harvest we did. In three months God lead 101 people to Himself through our family in India, and all out of our little kitchen! I think William Carey would have been proud.

We must understand that God is up to something significant in every generation, and He is exhorting His Church to get on board and get involved by understanding the season of the current generation.

Understanding Our Season Point #4

This is a season to harvest at a rate unprecedented in all of history!

We are seeing astronomical numbers come to Jesus in Africa through *Christ for All Nations* ministry and others. We are witnessing a major revival in Argentina through a house-church movement. And, what can we even say about what God is doing in countries like China, India, and South Korea?

Additionally, all we have to do in order to understand God's timing and what He is up to, is to look at our current society. It is a challenge for the average person to keep up with the complex advancements in technology. The advent of internet and wireless communications, together with other "signs of the times," has propelled us toward a consummation of history and the commencement of God's great outpouring.

Church history and world history both play out simultaneously under the direct orchestration of God's Spirit. God is ready to do the harvesting. Each generation of believers has had to discern what God is up to in their time and begin to invest wholeheartedly in that, and we can do the same today. Let's thrust in the sickle and reap! Time is short and there is much to do.

Testifying while Sanctifying

The Gospel does not, in any way, need to be complicated, and neither do its messengers. God delights to see people who love Him and believe in Him to live unpretentiously and on target.

Consider these words from Galatians 5:6, *"What is important is faith expressing itself in love."* Notice the simplicity of those words. Couldn't you get excited about jumping into something so simple, yet so supernatural? We don't have to be geniuses, or understand much of anything, except living lives of faith expressed through acts of love. It's when we complicate the message and make the process complex that we find so much trouble. God wants to clean us up and set us apart from the world. He desires holiness and purity and a complete abstaining from living for our flesh. That is made abundantly clear in His Word (II Corinthians 1:12, 6:19-20; Philippians 1:27; I Peter 1:16-17, 3:1; I John 3:7-10). He never intended for us to tuck and hide or to put our lives in neutral until we get "right". He has declared us to be righteous, and we are to live righteously every day as much as possible.

Let's look at the Bible to illustrate this further. In Acts 8:1-8 we see this with remarkable clarity.

1 Saul was one of the witnesses, and he agreed completely with the killing of Stephen. A great wave of persecution began that day, sweeping over the church in Jerusalem; and all the believers except the apostles were scattered through the regions of Judea and Samaria. 2 (Some devout men came and buried Stephen with great mourning.) 3 But Saul was going everywhere to destroy the church. He went from house to house, dragging out both men and women to throw them into prison. 4 But the believers who were scattered preached the Good News about Jesus wherever they went. 5 Philip, for example, went to the city of Samaria and told the people there about the Messiah. 6 Crowds listened intently to Philip because they were eager to hear his message and see the miraculous signs he did. 7 Many evil spirits were cast out, screaming as they left their victims. And many who had been paralyzed or lame were healed. 8So there was great joy in that city.

The new believers, though robustly persecuted, "preached the Good News about Jesus wherever they went." They weren't scared. They had confidence in their Savior and His cause no matter the outcome of their lives. It is at least probable that some in their group would not have passed a stringent ethics test in many of our leadership circles today. In other words, I'm sure they had not all reached perfection yet. They had to realize that holiness is not congruent with hiding and privacy does not produce purity.

Let's look at another section from the Bible – I Thessalonians 1:3-10:

3 As we pray to our God and Father about you, we think of your faithful work, your loving deeds, and the enduring hope you have because of our Lord Jesus Christ. 4 We know, dear brothers and sisters, that God loves you and has chosen you to be his own people. 5 For when we brought you the Good News, it was not only with words but also with power, for the Holy Spirit gave you full assurance that what we said was true. And you know of our concern for you from the way we lived when we were with you. 6 So you received the message with joy from the Holy Spirit in spite of the severe suffering it brought you. In this way, you imitated both us and the Lord. 7 As a result, you have become an example to all the believers in Greece—throughout both Macedonia and Achaia. 8 And now the word of the Lord is ringing out from you to people everywhere, even beyond Macedonia and Achaia, for wherever we go we find people telling us about your faith in God. We don't need to tell them about it, 9 for they keep talking about the wonderful welcome you gave us and how you turned away from idols to serve the living and true God. 10 And they speak of how you are looking forward to the coming of God's Son from Heaven – Jesus, whom God raised from the dead. He is the One who has rescued us from the terrors of the coming judgment.

Incredible! Look at these people. Notice their drive and determination to live their lives full of faith in order to advance the Gospel advancement. They did not waste time on "sanctification courses", they just sanctified while they testified.

God is looking for people who will put their lives into motion as they take seriously His demand for personal holiness. He does not enjoy seeing people living morally bankrupt lives, nor is He pleased when people who seemingly promote holiness don't exercise such holiness by reaching out to lost, hurting people. They grow fat on themselves while people perish—and this does not please our Master.

Another example from the Bible is illustrated in the life of the Apostle Peter. Remember him? Peter was one of the great leaders in the early church and one of the closest confidants of Jesus while He was on the earth. Peter was used mightily by God both in miracles and in preaching the Gospel. Peter wrote two letters that ended up becoming canonized as Holy Scripture. Peter, under the influence of the Holy Spirit, was as supernaturally gifted and anointed as they come. He would be a sure "Hall of Famer" in Christianity, if there was such a thing. Too often, however, Peter's acts of "greatness" are often overshadowed by some of his "screw-ups". These failures would probably have disqualified him for ministry today (not to mention the fact that he had no seminary training).

Let's roll a little through some of his prominent episodes, just through the book of Matthew, looking at both the good and the bad. Notice how often Jesus goes back to Peter after a big "screw up".

Good	**Bad**
Chosen by Christ to follow Him (Mt. 10:2)	Abandoned Jesus (Mt. 26:56)
Walks on water (Mt. 14:27-29)	Sank quickly (Mt.14:30)
Holy Spirit reveals that Jesus is Messiah(Mt. 16:13-16)	Satan speaks through him (Mt.16:22-23)
Becomes part of Jesus' inner circle (Mt. 17:1-7)	Can't understand spiritual things (Mt. 17:4)
Promises to never leave Christ (Mt. 26:33-37)	Denies Him and runs away (Mt. 26:69-75)
Gets to help Jesus in the Garden (Mt. 26:36-38)	Falls asleep instead (Mt. 26:40-41)

I'd just bet that Peter would love to forget the entire chapter of Matthew 26. Can you imagine if you were allowed such wonderful privileges by Christ and you failed miserably? What must have gone through his mind for so long?

Today, so many of us rail on Peter as some kind of failure-ridden, over-presumptuous, misfit, but we could ask ourselves several questions. When was the last time I lead 3,000 to Christ in one day? When was the last time I walked on water for even one yard? When was the last time I laid hands on sick and crippled people and they miraculously recovered? (Acts 3 and Acts 5:12-15) When was the last time I spoke in a different language so clearly that everyone could understand me, and I had never attended one language course? (Acts 2:1-5)

Also take note of what the religious leaders of that day said about Peter and the other apostles. (Acts 4:13) "The members of the council were amazed when they saw the boldness of Peter and John, for they could see that they were ordinary men with no special training in the Scriptures. They also recognized them as men who had been with Jesus."

We can, therefore, conclude that although Peter and many of the early followers of Christ dealt with sinful tendencies, they did not stop preaching the Gospel everywhere they went. They testified while they sanctified. We can, too.

It's about the Three E's

Having six children, I can tell you about the joys and struggles of parenting to some extent. One struggle is keeping our children on task, especially in the mornings when getting ready for school. They need frequent, gentle reminders every day to stay focused on the last thing we told them to do.

I believe that the Body of Christ struggles with the same thing. God has to keep giving those gentle reminders for us to stay focused on the things He has asked us to do. There are three things that would put us, the Body of Christ, in position to radically change the entire world in short order, if we incorporated all three in our lives at the same time. I call them the 3 E's. Every believer is called to:

Exalt the Lord

Psalm 96:1-4

1 Sing a new song to the Lord! Let the whole earth sing to the Lord! 2 Sing to the Lord; praise his name. Each day proclaim the good news that he saves. 3 Publish his glorious deeds among the nations. Tell everyone about the amazing things he does. 4 Great is the Lord! He is most worthy of praise! He is to be feared above all gods.

We were created to worship God and we ever live to make His Name known throughout the earth. That is our job, but actually it is our privilege. As missionaries to a lost world, the Church must realize that it exists to proclaim Jesus as Lord and exalt Him in everything we say and do.

We exalt the Lord in three ways:

The way we live (Proverbs 21:8)

"The guilty walk a crooked path; the innocent travel a straight road."

Someone once said, "The best sermon is the one seen, not heard." In other words, our lives are the billboards for advertising the goodness and holiness of the Lord. We do this by:

1.- Standing up with conviction;
2.- Standing ready with commitment; and
3.- Standing down to pride and hostility.

With our mouth (Psalm 51:15)

"Unseal my lips, O Lord that my mouth may praise You."

God will give us many opportunities to speak for Him to lost people. We have to be willing to take advantage of those opportunities. We can choose to exalt Jesus with our verbal *stance* or deny Him with our verbal *collapse*. Here are some thoughts to consider:

1.- People who praise God in private live much better lives publicly.
2.- Practicing praise at home makes it easier to do so in public.
3.- We must deal with our issues of being ashamed of Jesus.

By learning to tell your/His story (Psalm 145:4)

"Let each generation tell its children of your mighty acts;
let them proclaim your power."

There's an old saying, "A picture is like a thousand words and an experience is like a thousand pictures." No one knows what God did for you quite like you do. God gives you a wonderful redemptive history in order to be able to tell others how they can see their history rewritten. The best way to tell your/His story is:

1.- Keep it simple and to the point;
2.- Tell the facts of what Jesus did for you; and
3.- Sell it like you mean it.

Encourage Believers

Hebrews 10:24

"Let us think of ways to motivate one another to acts of love
and good works"

One of the most rewarding assignments we have as believers is to intentionally and assertively encourage each other. Just picture it—attending church service with the expressed purpose of bringing encouragement to fellow believers, thereby motivating them to further render acts of kindness to others. What a wonderful utopia! I believe, however, that many attend churches in order to "get something" from the service or simply fulfill what they feel is their "Christian duty". Neither of these reasons demonstrates love or encouragement.

Additionally, there may be some who feel that they are just called to worship God alone and stay at home. These people create a false sense of security, forgetting that what they are exemplifying by doing this is utter selfishness. If they aren't attending church with the intent of encouraging other believers, they are seriously short changing the Body of Christ. They are leaving an "encouragement vacuum" that cannot be filled. Consequently, such passivity breeds rebellion and disregard for authority, bringing a compound fracture to the Christian community.

Is it hard to stay committed to encouraging the Body? Of course it is, because the Body of Christ is made up of people just like you and me who have tendencies to fail, to be fickle, and to be fragile. We are susceptible to struggle some days just to make the grade socially, economically, and even spiritually. Following are some encouraging suggestions to apply when we see those around us struggling:

1.- Soften your heart.
2.- Give people the same break you hope for each day.
3.- Allow people on the front end "room to fail".
4.- Refuse and diffuse any fuse and choose to lose.

Evangelize the Lost

Of course, this third E is the propellant of this book. When we are exalting the Lord passionately and unashamedly with exciting praise and intimate worship, we bring honor to the Lord. When we set our hearts to enthusiastically encourage every believer we can, we bring honor to the Lord. Consequently, when we reach out with the Gospel to lost people, we bring honor to the Lord.

The key is to do each one of the 3 E's simultaneously and with the same amount of energy exhibited for each. We cannot do one without the other; we dare not try. The Lord of the harvest today awaits our reply.

Chapter Four

Striking out into the Realm of Faith, Fire, and Adventure

"I have but one candle of life to burn, and I would burn it out in a land filled with darkness than in a land flooded with light."

John Falconer

I'll never forget the day I first met him. With his broad shoulders squared, he approached me with a sure and unequaled confidence that immediately grabbed my attention. His eyes were the most sincere and searching I had ever seen. When stirred by a person's need, his eyes filled with tears so quickly that they seemed to be on a timer. His face was flooded with such genuine concern that he made you feel important and significant. His smile seemed as healthy as wheat bread and as contagious as the flu. He grinned widely, laughed robustly, and hugged with sincerity and strength.

The very minute Nagash Gemelial greeted me, he hugged me tight and said, "Praise God for you dear brother! You are a blessing from God!" Though this was the first time I met him, I felt an indisputable kinship with him. I had only heard stories about him from my friend Patrick of IOI, but now the stories began to come alive.

Some months later, I went to meet with Nagash in Ethiopia, his home country, and it was much more of the same thing as our earlier meeting. Quite frankly, I was in awe of him because of his enviably intimate walk with Jesus, and he treated everyone as if they were the only person in the world. When he prayed, Nagash didn't just pray, he cried! His prayers got right to the point and shot right to the heart. He prayed about everything and gave honor to Jesus with nearly each syllable he uttered.

He also had a determined purpose that seemed to raise him above his normal surroundings. Nagash had a faith walk that was as exciting and pure as few who came before him. He just knew that God was up to something and he was not going to be left out. Nagash Gemeliel taught me so much in such a little time; I felt like I had taken a crash course in real Christianity just by being around him.

Nagash believes in living out the red letters of the Bible. He doesn't seem to get involved in any conversation, any activity, anything that does not draw him and others closer to the Savior. This kind of living makes arrogant men crumble and humble men have hope. He takes Jesus at His word and then moves forward with quiet, yet fiery resolve to accomplish it despite what others may do.

It was on this trip to Ethiopia that the Lord used Nagash in a powerful way in my life personally. I was praying for one of the many missionaries that he and *Indigenous Outreach International* support, when Nagash suddenly looked up at me and interrupted my praying to speak a word from the Lord to me. He said, "Brother, there is a fire in you that is strong, but it has grown weak. You need to keep it burning and let that fire consume you and others." His words went straight into my heart. I had been pining away in spiritual "cool down" for the last year. Due somewhat to some spiritual laziness on my part and being in dead, cold religious surroundings, I had allowed the fire of God to become secondary. I never recognized that I was losing it. I thought of myself as a pretty enthusiastic Christian, as many had even described me. But the passion for Jesus Christ was not the greatest passion of my life. Nagash heard from the Lord and spoke the truth in love to me.

As I returned from his homeland to mine, I sensed God speaking deeply in my soul that I could not continue to supplant my faith with double-minded and distracted mindsets. It was now time to return to the miraculous and powerful; quite simply put, the life of faith in God. I had to be brave, but I knew that whatever was to come my way in the form of persecution would be so insignificant compared to the great benefits I and many others would receive. Bring on the faith! Bring on the fire! Bring on the adventure!

It's Time to Fill up the Boat

Revelation 14:14-16

14 Then I saw a white cloud, and seated on the cloud was someone like the Son of Man. He had a gold crown on His head and a sharp sickle in His hand. 15 Then another angel came from the Temple and shouted to the One sitting on the cloud, "Swing the sickle, for the time of harvest has come, the crop on earth is ripe!" 16 So the One sitting on the cloud swung His sickle over the earth, and the whole earth was harvested.

Recently, I had the opportunity to hear, in person, the great evangelist Reinhard Bonnke. Believe me, he is incredible and is the same in person as he is on video. He has one passion—souls! Bonnke recounted a vision that he had many years earlier, long before he ever witnessed crowds in excess of 1,000,000 responding to the Gospel at one time. The vision helped launch his ministry and his undeniable zeal for the lost.

In the vision Bonnke was standing in a boat and recognized that his lone companion in that boat was his Savior, Jesus. With fondness he looked over at Jesus in the boat with him. Jesus did not speak, but simply looked down into the water and pointed. Bonnke followed Jesus' example and also looked over the side of the boat into the water. Much to his surprise, the water was completely black. This puzzled him so he looked more closely, and this time noticed that the water was not water at all, but a sea of people—all Africans. Jesus looked at Bonnke, gesturing only with His eyes a plea for help. Bonnke immediately began to throw life preservers into the water and each preserver hauled in hundreds of people. As he hurriedly continued this task, he noticed the boat was immensely expanding as people were pulled on board.

Then, just like that, the vision was over. Bonnke knew what to do, however, and began an incredible faith-filled journey to see all of Africa saved! His journey took him and has continued to take him from tiny Lesotho to much of the entire continent of Africa and around the world in search of lost people. He has determined to throw out the nets for as big of catch as God will give him. And throw out the nets he has. This one evangelist, and his wonderful team of *Christ for All Nations,* is on a course to win 100 million souls in the first decade of the new century! We are not far from 2010 and already Bonnke and his team are close to that goal.

God has opened up the continent of Africa to the Gospel as unprecedented in all of history. God is demonstrating through *Christ for All Nations* precisely what we have talked about in this book—time is of the essence to gather souls into God's Kingdom. He wants us to pull in every person we meet to fill up every crack and crevice of our boats as He supernaturally creates expansion to add even more. He can and will do His part; He desperately wants us to do ours.

Luke 14:23

"Go out into the country lanes and behind the hedges and urge anyone you find to come, so that the house will be full."

Just like in Bonnke's dream, the more we go looking for them and the more we pull them in, the more room He will make for them. It's time to fill up the ever-expanding boat! I've always been fascinated by the story in Luke 5:1-11:

1 One day as Jesus was preaching on the shore of the Sea of Galilee, great crowds pressed in on him to listen to the word of God. 2 He noticed two empty boats at the water's edge, for the fishermen had left them and were washing their nets. 3 Stepping into one of the boats, Jesus asked Simon, its owner, to push it out into the water. So he sat in the boat and taught the crowds from there. 4 When he had finished speaking, he said to Simon, "Now go out where it is deeper, and let down your nets to catch some fish." 5 "Master," Simon replied, "we worked hard all last night and didn't catch a thing. But if you say so, I'll let the nets down again." 6 And this time their nets were so full of fish they began to tear! 7 A shout for help brought their partners in the other boat, and soon both boats were filled with fish and on the verge of sinking. 8 When Simon Peter realized what had happened, he fell to his knees before Jesus and said, "Oh, Lord, please leave me—I'm too much of a sinner to be around you." 9 For he was awestruck by the number of fish they had caught, as were the others with him. 10 His partners, James and John, the sons of Zebedee, were also amazed. Jesus replied to Simon, "Don't be afraid! From now on you'll be fishing for people!" 11 And as soon as they landed, they left everything and followed Jesus.

What an incredible scene! Can you imagine, husbands and fathers, if this were you? We cannot simply gloss over the narrative in the Bible and not discover the amazing relevancy that lives in that narrative.

First of all, we must realize that Simon Peter was one thing, a fisherman. He worked hard just like most Galileans to eek out a meager living. He probably had little or no discretionary income that wasn't taken by Roman taxes under Herod. His family had lived under both poverty and tyranny for years. I can imagine that he probably worked countless extra hours at the behest of his wife and comrades. *Verse 5: "Master, we've worked hard all last night…"* After rereading this account, it's probably a safe bet that Peter was also often frustrated.

Then, suddenly, one day the Phenom of Phenoms walks up to the shoreline. He comes to these hardworking fishermen to borrow their boat for awhile so He could preach. What? What audacity and insensitivity! Doesn't He recognize who He is addressing and how long they have labored? They work hard at fishing, so it is thought, because they can't get an education and learn under the Rabbi like it appeared Jesus must have done. These men, who were uneducated and probably illiterate, had to be reduced to working their hands and feet to the bone while this man, this preacher, could just walk around and talk to people about life. Now He's asking to use their boat to do some of his "preaching".

For whatever reason, they agreed to His request. Then audacity turns to insanity in their minds, I'm sure, as Jesus begins instructing them on how to fish. *Verse 4: "When Jesus had finished speaking, He said to Simon, 'Now, go out where it is deeper, and let down your nets to catch some fish.'"* This should have been a breaking point for Simon Peter. It doesn't say, but I'll bet he was getting a little tired of some local rabbi running a show that was his to run. The story just gets more intriguing, however, from here.

Suddenly, the unimaginable happens! Fish start jumping into these fishermen's nets as never before. These professional fishermen had only dreamed of such a catch, and now they were having to team up to bring it all in. *Verses 6-: "And this time their nets began to tear! A shout for help brought their partners in the other boat and soon both boats were filled with fish and on the verge of sinking."*

Just a little side-note: Whenever you trust God and launch out for Him, He will rock your world with His awesome provision. There will more about this later.

Well, so now what was Peter to think? All of his anger and arrogance had been swallowed up by a miracle, Peter's whole life is now flashing before his very eyes. Everything that he had ever known and held dear was about to come crashing down, only to be replaced with the unthinkable. Once again, it's just like God to do that.

So, I can see it now. There were all these old salty dogs standing around holding their nets and staring in disbelief at the abundance of fish now in their boats. Peter stood, staring at Jesus. What did he see in that moment in the eyes of the Messiah? Was he beginning to realize that the way he thought about things up to that point might have been wrong? What kind of emotion was he experiencing at that moment? We see a little bit of the answer in his response to Jesus in verses 8-9: *"When Simon Peter realized what had happened, he fell to his knees before Jesus and said, 'Oh Lord, please leave me – I'm too much of a sinner to be around you!' For he was awestruck by the number of fish they had caught, as were the others with him."*

Now, let's pause the tape here for a moment and step back and look at what we have. We have a bunch of poor, uneducated, going nowhere fishermen, who have been struggling in life just to survive. Suddenly, their lifelong dream had come true—their ships were overflowing with fish. That which they had trained for and lived for since they were little boys, that which they had probably promised to their wives because of their expertise on the sea, and that to which they had devoted life and limb to accomplish had been fulfilled that day.

This is the part of the story where Ed McMahon comes up to the door with a camera crew, balloons, and a huge check for some Publisher's Clearing House winner. This is the part where most people would stop and say, "Oh, if I could only have a million dollars, my life would be great!"

The response of these fishermen will leave you in awe. *Versus 10 and 11: "Jesus replied to Simon, 'Don't be afraid! From now on you'll be fishing for people.' And as soon as they landed, they left everything and followed Jesus."*

What?!? You mean to say they left the huge catch of fish right there? You mean to say they walked away from something they had dreamed of for years? YES, that is exactly what they did. They accepted the plan offered by the Person who granted them the culmination of their dreams. He handed them two boatloads of fish and then simply challenged them with a greater dream. As He walked away, they chose to chase right behind, leaving the spoils of generations of fishing dreams right there on the seashore for others to pick up and enjoy.

How many of us would have done that? How many of us would give up everything in a moment's notice in order to chase the Great Giver of Dreams. Well, just in case you are one of those who might be ready to do so, here are some encouraging and challenging proposals for you:

Walk away from your dream.

We all start out not knowing what we want to do with our lives. Only a few of us are absolutely sure what we want to do when we grow up. Oh, but after listening through the years to our parents and/or peers, we begin to develop ambitions toward a specific career. It's then that we get ready to head off to college to get a jump start on fulfilling that dream. At this point we seem invincible and ready to "be somebody". The most common reason our ambitions are even interrupted is due to the lack of money or support.

Our dreams often leave us searching beyond what they provide for us. We bounce from one idea to another, hoping to find that certain "something" that makes us feel significant and fulfilled, but to no avail. Why? The answer lies in the fact that we weren't meant to find fulfillment in the things of this world; therefore, we should look to our Father for the path He specifically designed for each of us.

Start living after God's dream.

Let's stop a minute and think: have we ever thought about what dream God has purposed for us? Why did He create us? What specific niche or niches did He design us to fulfill? I strongly believe that God is waiting on the other side of our choice to walk away from our own dreams to give us what He has dreamed for us all along. It's then that we will truly start to live and truly start to dream.

God knows each of us up close and personal and has a unique purpose for each of our lives. All we have to do is *discover* what that is, *dedicate* ourselves to it, and then *deliver* on our commitment to follow through with it.

Get your fishing license before any other license.

These days, in trying to carry out God's ordained mission to make disciples of every nation, we must become experts at fishing for the souls of men. I'm amazed at all the certificates, awards, degrees, and licenses we get, but fail to become good at the one thing Jesus said we would do—fish.

In God's kingdom, those who humble themselves before Him, forsake their own pursuits, and abandon themselves to His call, become experts at what makes God smile the most. If real fulfillment is what you desire, try going fishing—for souls.

Throw out the nets God gives you quickly and accurately.

When it comes to evangelism and missions, not all of us are gifted the same and not all of us are called to do the exact same thing. However, at the very moment our individual gifts and callings are revealed to us, we should respond immediately without delay. We have already learned that there is an urgency to participate in God's plan for mankind. In any emergency the best teams that respond and "save the day" are comprised of people who perform in the capacity they were specifically gifted and/or trained to do.

If everyone is trying to do the other's job, there is confusion, disorder, and delay in the midst of the emergency. Our local churches would do well to recognize this and train, equip, and place people for evangelism and missions in the area where they fit the best.

Peter didn't have it all together; neither did the other disciples. They learned, however, to adapt to Jesus' life and ministry, ever keeping that first call issued by Him that day on the shoreline of the Sea of Galilee— *"From now on you will fish for people."* Hey, that's a great idea! Let's join those classic fishermen in the same pursuit. I'll just bet we'll be the ones who benefit the greatest.

Faith Launched Missions

Acts 6:1-5

1 But as the believers rapidly multiplied, there were rumblings of discontent. The Greek-speaking believers complained about the Hebrew-speaking believers, saying that their widows were being discriminated against in the daily distribution of food. 2 So the Twelve called a meeting of all the believers. They said, "We apostles should spend our time teaching the word of God, not running a food program. 3 And so, brothers, select seven men who are well respected and are full of the Spirit and wisdom. We will give them this responsibility. 4 Then we apostles can spend our time in prayer and teaching the word." 5 Everyone liked this idea, and they chose the following: Stephen (a man full of faith and the Holy Spirit), Philip, Procorus, Nicanor, Timon, Parmenas, and Nicolas of Antioch (an earlier convert to the Jewish faith).

The first martyr that the Christian church ever recorded was a young man named Stephen. Not much is known about this incredible hero of faith except what we read in chapters 6 and 7 of Acts. We do know, though, from the description in the above passages, he was well known as a respected man "full of faith and the Spirit". He was chosen for a missional task by the church leaders, not because of pedigree or training, but because he was faithful and full of faith. I strongly believe that these two qualities should be synonymous with any individual, family, team, or church that desires to make an impact in missions because I believe that missions is all about *faithfulness* (to God's call) and *faith* (in God's ability and cause).

As you and your church begin to set your sights on fulfilling the Great Commission, remember that this journey is going to be one full of issues that affect faithfulness and challenges that work against faith.

We cannot afford to wait until we discover whether or not we qualify—WE MUST GET QUALIFIED. The line isn't as long as we might think for those signing up for a missional journey of faith. It's hard. It's lonely. It's not at all popular with religious people (note the outcome of Stephen), but it is worth it, because Jesus is worth it.

Hebrews 11:1-6

1 Faith is the confidence that what we hope for will actually happen; it gives us assurance about things we cannot see. 2 Through their faith, the people in days of old earned a good reputation. 3 By faith we understand that the entire universe was formed at God's command, that what we now see did not come from anything that can be seen. 4 It was by faith that Abel brought a more acceptable offering to God than Cain did. Abel's offering gave evidence that he was a righteous man, and God showed his approval of his gifts. Although Abel is long dead, he still speaks to us by his example of faith. 5 It was by faith that Enoch was taken up to heaven without dying—"he disappeared, because God took him."[a] For before he was taken up, he was known as a person who pleased God. 6 And it is impossible to please God without faith. Anyone who wants to come to him must believe that God exists and that he rewards those who sincerely seek him.

The ancients, who were ultra faithful to God, did nothing without faith, and consequently, commended highly for it. They understood that the invisible God, although He demonstrates His attributes through nature and the cosmos (Acts 17:24-31), was not one to "put on a show" to impress people. He must be discovered by those looking for Him with eyes of faith. In other words, we must believe without seeing.

Are you impressing the Lord with your faith? Remember, nothing impresses Him like it. Nothing gets His involvement like the duo of faith and obedience. God is looking over the horizons of our lives and exacting a little bit more faith out of each of us in order to bring us to the grandest adventures this life can offer.

Just think of a life without it. Though we might be able to order every aspect of our lives and live in quasi-peace, the truth is we're missing the abundance of true peace that God offers to each of us. He is prodding us along and speaking into our ears to trust Him and take a step. That "step" when taken as a result of true faith in God and His abilities, will result in a *launch*. You will be catapulted toward true living and true fulfillment. But, it all starts with a step.

Perhaps you are a church leader or part of a leadership team and you have been enjoying this book. I want to encourage you, don't just read this book—take a step! Take your leadership team through a faith journey together, confirming your purpose for sending missionaries as one of your main priorities. Don't allow the quicksand of religious requirements keep you and your team from doing this. Don't say, "That just isn't our personality." If that's the case, get a new one!

The Abuses of Faith vs. the Benefits of Faith

Yes, there are abuses of faith. It's sad to say, but people use "faith" to coerce and promote personal agendas. Remember, however, no matter what abuses you have seen in faith circles, you don't throw out the baby with the bath water. This Christian life is all about faith and the continuation thereof. Because of faith, we become more faithful to the everyday standards of life. We become better spouses and parents. We become better church members and community leaders, all when we live our lives full of faith. Faith is *exciting*, but it is also *stabilizing*. Faith requires steps of action and obedience.

Someone once told me, "I don't like those 'faith people' because they are so heavenly-minded that they are no earthly good." Although I understand what the person was trying to say (faith talkers are weird), he couldn't have been further from the truth. When you see someone who is connected to heaven and eternity by genuine faith, they are great motivators and thinkers, and they are some of the most faithful and productive people on the planet. The ones who do not exemplify this are either living *fake faith* or *faith in faith.*

Those who have faith in faith have set their focus on the wrong thing. We aren't mandated by God to believe in circumstances or in our abilities. When we put our faith in faith, we are trying to usurp God's *sovereignty* and invoke our *culpability.* We take it as our fault if normal "life situations" occur, thinking that we didn't "give it enough faith or faith confession." This is simply not true and it is not true faith.

True faith is *faith in God*—nothing else. It is not in our *confession,* but in our *reception.* We receive God, we don't conjure Him up. He is not a magic wand. He is the Creator of everything. We believe that He exists and that He will reward us (on His terms) as we diligently seek Him. This means that we are constantly reaching *up* and not *in.* We are not exercising ourselves to death over whether our goals or agendas are met. Instead, we are jumping into our Beloved's hands and living to worship Him. He will do all the *impossible* unseen work while we do our *possible.* We trust and obey Him wholeheartedly, and He does the rest!

Take chances for eternal rewards (Acts 20:18-27)

When we look at the life and ministry of Paul, the great apostle, evangelist, and missionary, we tend to think of him as a superstar Christian. He was, without a doubt, one of the greatest examples of an "Evangelical Christian" we could ever hear about. However, though he did receive a special call from God, we should not think that we have not received the same. We are to live our lives with the same urgency and propriety that he did. No believer is exempt by God from laying their lives down for Jesus. True

121

believers in every century since Christ have felt compelled to lay down their fears and take chances in this life in order to see the rewards in the life to come.

Hebrews 11:32-40

32 Now much more do I need to say? It would take too long to recount the stories of the faith of Gideon, Barak, Samson, Jephthah, David, Samuel, and all the prophets. 33 By faith these people overthrew kingdoms, ruled with justice, and received what God had promised them. They shut the mouths of lions, 34 quenched the flames of fire, and escaped death by the edge of the sword. Their weakness was turned to strength. They became strong in battle and put whole armies to flight. 35 Women received their loved ones back again from death. But others were tortured, refusing to turn from God in order to be set free. They placed their hope in a better life after the resurrection. 36 Some were jeered at, and their backs were cut open with whips. Others were chained in prisons. 37 Some died by stoning, some were sawed in half, and others were killed with the sword. Some went about wearing skins of sheep and goats, destitute and oppressed and mistreated. 38 They were too good for this world, wandering over deserts and mountains, hiding in caves and holes in the ground. 39 All these people earned a good reputation because of their faith, yet none of them received all that God had promised. 40 For God had something better in mind for us, so that they would not reach perfection without us.

Why do we ever need to take chances? Why should we ever be asked to give up our lives? Isn't just living with Jesus in our hearts enough? Can't we simply believe in Him and let the other pieces fall into place? Some belief systems in Christianity answer those questions by fostering perpetual inactivity and complacency. They maintain that believing in Jesus is all we need to do and He will take care of the rest.

It is true that belief in Jesus is all we need for salvation; BUT, what do we do with the nagging of the Great Commission which stands as a huge wall of opposition to our complacency? What do we do when the Holy Spirit repeats His plea in our hearts to step out of our comfort zones and reach out to those who have never heard of Him? I definitely agree that we are called to enter "the rest" promised by God in Hebrews 4:1-3; because we then cease to "strive" in our own righteousness. This passage is not one that suggests we sit down and fold our arms across our chests, but in reality strongly advocates that we actively live our lives to advance the Kingdom of God as proof that we have entered that rest. We must keep the whole of God's Word and His nature in context.

Choose to launch.

"You are Go for Launch"

Those words, so often used by launch command in Cape Canaveral, Florida, are the stirring prerequisites to the many space shuttle and rocket launches used since the 1960s. Today, we are using them with the same spirit of drama and action for your ministry, because it's time to set your sights on God's awesome impossible dream. No person can pull off this ministry quite the way you can. No person is more deeply entrenched in the beginning dynamics of this particular ministry than you. You have been called by God, well-trained and equipped, intensely inspired, and genuinely encouraged. Now it's simply a matter of WILL YOU LAUNCH?

Jet boosters are ready, all systems go, the vast expanse of unlimited mission opportunities await. The grandstands are hushed, filled with people enthusiastically anticipating the inevitable forthcoming adventure. The field is set for a great show, but the question is WILL YOU LAUNCH?

The decision rests with you. The best intentions fall miles short of the least bit of action. Great intentions never fed a hungry mouth or healed the sick, or put an end to suffering and misery. Although motivated by intention, those things were only accomplished on the stage of "action". So many people live in the chamber of the gun, filled with the gunpowder of the Holy Spirit and the Word of God, yet refuse to enter the barrel to be fired. This is called FEAR OF THE TRIGGER. Do you face this fear?

There has never been a more crucial time to minister for Jesus. Why? Because, we live today in a world so chaotic that the remnant which venture into the great swell seem disproportionately inundated with needs and opportunities which keep them working tirelessly without an end. The deck is always stacked and the players are constantly being rigorously shuffled and empirically dealt. The event of the ages is right upon us and God is looking for us, the new players, to respond.

I dedicate this book to my beautiful and wonderful wife, Amy, who is my true hero in life, a true missionary, and the most influential person I know. I can't live this life without you.

I also dedicate this book to my six wonderful children, Jon, Julia, Stephen, Victoria, Nathan, and Sara. I love you and thank you for believing in your Daddy. I can't live this life without you either.

I love and need you.

Bibliography

All Scripture verses from the *New Living Translation* except where noted. Tyndale House Publishers – Copyright 1996

Quotations from Reinhard Bonnke
   Words Like Fire The Passion and Wisdom of a Lifetime of Soul-Winning
   Christ For All Nations – Copyright 2008

All other quotations
   Famous Christian Quotes – www.project 1615.org/quotes

LaVergne, TN USA
11 December 2009
166699LV00004B/5/P